FEATHERED STAR

NEW QUILTS
from an OLD FAVORITE

American Quilter's Society

P. O. Box 3290 • Paducah, KY 42002-3290
FAX 270-898-1173 www.AQSquilt.com

Located in Paducah, Kentucky, the American Quilter's Society (AQS) is dedicated to promoting the accomplishments of today's quilters. Through its publications and events, AQS strives to honor today's quiltmakers and their work and to inspire future creativity and innovation in quiltmaking.

EDITORS: BARBARA SMITH & SHELLEY HAWKINS
GRAPHIC DESIGN: LYNDA SMITH
COVER DESIGN: MICHAEL BUCKINGHAM
PHOTOGRAPHY: CHARLES R. LYNCH

Feathered star / (editor, Barbara Smith].
    p. cm. -- (New quilts from an old favorite)
    ISBN 1-57432-817-4
    1. Patchwork--Patterns. 2. Patchwork quilts--Competitions--United
States. 3. Star quilts--United States. I. Smith, Barbara 1941- II.
American Quilter's Society. III. Series

TT835.F42 2003
    746.46'041--dc21
        2003003826

Additional copies of this book may be ordered from the American Quilter's Society, PO Box 3290, Paducah, KY 42002-3290; 800-626-5420 (orders only please); or online at www.AQSquilt.com. For all other inquiries, call 270-898-7903.

Dedication

This book is dedicated to all those who view a
traditional quilt block and see within it a link to
the past and a vision for the future.

The Museum of the American Quilter's Society (MAQS)

An exciting place where the public can learn more
about quilts, quiltmaking, and quiltmakers.

Through collecting quilts and other programs,
MAQS focuses on celebrating and developing today's quiltmaking.

Whether presenting new or antique quilts, MAQS promotes understanding of,
and respect for, all quilts – new and antique, traditional and innovative,
machine made and hand made, utility and art.

Contents

Preface

While preservation of the past is a museum's primary function, its greatest service is performed as it links the past to the present and to the future. With that intention, the Museum of the American Quilter's Society (MAQS) sponsors an annual contest and exhibit called *New Quilts from an Old Favorite*.

Created to acknowledge our quiltmaking heritage and to recognize innovation, creativity, and excellence, the contest challenges today's quiltmakers to interpret a single traditional quilt block in a work of their own design. Each year contestants respond with a myriad of stunning interpretations.

Feathered Star: New Quilts from an Old Favorite is a wonderful representation of these interpretations. In this book you'll find a brief description of the 2003 contest, followed by a presentation of the five award winners and the thirteen finalists and their quilts.

Full-color photographs of the quilts accompany each quiltmaker's comments – comments that provide insight into their widely diverse creative processes. Full-sized templates for the traditional Feathered Star block are included to form the basis for your own rendition. Tips, techniques, and patterns contributed by the contest winners offer an artistic framework for your own design.

Our wish is that *Feathered Star: New Quilts from an Old Favorite* will further our quiltmaking heritage as new quilts based on the Feathered Star block are inspired by the outstanding quilts, patterns, and instructions in this book.

The Contest

The annual MAQS contest, *New Quilts from an Old Favorite*, challenges quilt-makers to create unconventional and innovative quilts from a single traditional block pattern. The 2003 contest theme was the Feathered Star block, and quilt-makers from around the world responded to the challenge.

The following were basic requirements for entries:

- Quilts were to be recognizable in some way as being related to the Feathered Star block.
- The finished size of the quilt was to be a minimum of 50" in width and height but could not exceed 100".
- Quilting was required on each quilt.
- A quilt could be entered only by the person(s) who made it.
- Each entry must have been completed after December 31, 1997.

Each quiltmaker was asked to submit an entry form and two slides of their quilt – one of the full quilt, and a second of a detail from the piece. Three jurors viewed dozens of slides, deliberating over design, use of materials, interpretation of the theme, and technical excellence, narrowing the field of entries to eighteen finalists who were invited to submit their quilts for judging.

With quilts by the eighteen finalists gathered, three judges meticulously examined the pieces, evaluating them again for design, innovation, theme, and workmanship. First-place through fifth-place award winners were selected and notified.

Each year, the *New Quilts from an Old Favorite* contest winners and finalists are featured in an exhibit that opens at the Museum of the American Quilter's Society in Paducah, Kentucky. Over a two-year period, the exhibit travels to a number of museums across North America and is viewed by thousands of quilt enthusiasts. Corporate sponsorship of the contest helps to underwrite costs, enabling even smaller museums across the country to display the exhibit. They are also included in a beautiful book published by the American Quilter's Society. *Feathered Star: New Quilts from an Old Favorite* is the tenth in the contest, exhibit, and publication series. Other block designs used as contest themes include: Double Wedding Ring, Log Cabin, Ohio Star, Mariner's Compass, Pineapple Quilts, Kaleidoscope, Storm at Sea, Bear's Paw, and Tumbling Blocks.

For information about entering the current year's *New Quilts from an Old Favorite* contest, write to the Museum of the American Quilter's Society at PO Box 1540, Paducah, KY, 42002-1540; call (270) 442-8856; or visit MAQS online at www.quiltmuseum.org.

Feathered Star Block

From basic to baroque, the Feathered Star design turns the ordinary into the extraordinary. Many of the stars are based on a simple design, such as an unequal Nine-Patch, then trimmed with small triangles, making the Feathered Star an intricate yet beloved pattern among quiltmakers.

One of the oldest designs in quilt history, Feathered Star quilts are revered for their heirloom quality. Mastery of this patchwork pattern can be considered the peak of quiltmaking expertise. Although piecing this block has become easier and more precise than in early days, the complexity of the pattern results from the many small pieces the block contains.

The composition of the Feathered Star offers endless variations in the design. Blazing Star, Pine Cone, Star of Chamblie, Star of Bethlehem, Octagonal Star, and Star Spangled Banner are just a few familiar variations. The large center of the pattern's unequal Nine-Patch provides an excellent area for creative distinction. The center can be filled with a LeMoyne Star, Nine-Patch, Blazing Sun, Flying Geese, or any other design that is enhanced when framed by feathers.

From curved piecing to appliqué and traditional to contemporary, the winners and finalists in the Feathered Star contest expand the artistic possibilities of the design while maintaining its grandeur. Each quilt represents a pinnacle in the galaxy of Feathered Star designs

Sherri Bain Driver

Englewood, Colorado

My work is in a variety of styles. If you saw all my quilts together, you might have a hard time believing they were made by just one person.

MEET THE QUILTER

With an interest in fabric and sewing from an early age, I learned to sew as a child, making most of my own clothes. Through the years I've tried counted cross-stitch, needlepoint, crewel, and smocking. While these crafts were enjoyable, none of them kept my interest for long. In experimenting with needlework, I made a few quilts.

It was not until 1987, when involved in several quilting organizations, that I became hooked. That year, some friends formed a quilt guild as well as an informal bee that met weekly. The bee has changed quite a bit through the years, but I'm still a member of the group and our friendships are strong. I started quilting as an outlet for creative expression, but found something unexpected – a community of quilters who became my dearest friends.

Quiltmaking began as a hobby for me, but soon became more. I've taught quilting classes, designed quilts and patterns, and written two books. I am a quilt judge certified by the National Quilting Association and am currently a full-time editor for a quilting magazine. I still make time to teach occasionally, and make a few quilts each year.

My work is in a variety of styles. If you saw all my quilts together, you might not believe they were made by one person. I love old-fashioned traditional quilts, cutting-edge contemporary quilts, and everything in between, but my favorite way to work is making innovative changes to a traditional design. This is the fourth time one of my quilts has been juried into the MAQS contest.

Native Weavings: Feathered Star

57" x 57"

I look forward to working with the design MAQS chooses for the contest each year. I usually begin by making hand or computer sketches until something interesting develops. Typically, I start with an idea for the center of the quilt and work out the rest of the design as the quilt develops. Not planning all the details before starting produces some fun surprises.

For the MAQS contests, I begin sketching as soon as the holidays are over, start cutting and sewing in mid-summer, and usually finish my quilt just before the deadline. The pressure of a deadline helps me finish! My quilts usually begin with a stack of fabric I'm crazy about and a rough idea of what to make. The Feathered Star idea was already decided, so I just had to pick which stack of beautiful fabrics to use.

I've fallen in love with ikat fabrics and buy them whenever possible. At one time, they were available in chain fabric stores, but now it takes some effort to find them. I look for ikats in the vendor booths at quilt shows and in specialty shops. Sometimes clothes and other items made from ikats, such as shirts, shorts, and tablecloths, can be cut up and made into quilts. The group of fabrics in this quilt includes an exotic ikat from a miniskirt I bought while vacationing in Honduras, knowing that it would become part of a quilt rather than my wardrobe. The fabrics also include a fascinating spiral tie-dyed medallion by Ricky Tims and a hand-dyed fabric from my friend, Janet Jo Smith.

I've made several Feathered Stars with traditional patterns and techniques. For this quilt, I thought it would be interesting to make the feathers without half-square triangles but didn't know how to accomplish this. It was not until browsing through a magazine on American Indian art and finding a small photo of an intricately patterned coiled basket that the solution occurred to me. I immediately realized that the Feathered Star could be drafted in a circle, and the spaces between the star points filled with curves. The little triangular feathers could be added to the ends of the curves with the stitch-and-flip technique. Many years ago, I had taken a class from June Ryker, who wrote patterns and taught classes for making curved Log Cabin quilts. At that time, my skills didn't allow me to successfully complete a project, but I learned the concept of sewing bias strips to a foundation. As soon as I saw the coiled basket, I knew June's technique could be used to create curves for my quilt.

I made a rough sketch of my mental design containing a large circle with an eight-pointed star. Because I usually plan only the center of the quilt, the fabrics and the developing quilt guide the design from there. If I knew what a quilt would look like before starting to sew, I'd never bother to make it. It's nice to be surprised and challenged along the way.

Making It Up As You Go

I love to make decisions as the quilt progresses rather than create a complete plan before starting a quilt. It requires spending more time pondering and auditioning fabrics and design possibilities than sewing, but I love working like this.

FULL-SIZED PAPER PATTERN

For a complicated design, I like to make a full-sized paper pattern, sometimes cutting it up as I go, other times making a master drawing to keep intact and use as a sewing guide. A freezer-paper pattern can be cut up as the quilt is constructed and the pieces used as iron-on templates or foundations, as needed. In the past, I have sometimes had problems getting pieces to fit. With a full-sized pattern drawn on a single piece of paper, I can be sure the pieces will fit back together. After all, if it began as one flat piece, with careful sewing, it should come together to make a flat quilt.

Another advantage of making a full-sized pattern is the ability to draw the parts I'm sure of, then fill in the rest as the quilt develops. A design that looks good in a sketch might not work with specific fabrics.

For this quilt, I began by taping several pieces of freezer paper together to make a large square. Working on the unfinished cement floor in my basement, I used a yardstick compass to draw a large circle in the square, marked diagonals to find the circle's center, then drew an eight-pointed star in the circle. Knowing that I wanted to divide the star points to make a more complex kaleidoscopic center, the star points were drawn fairly large. The yardstick compass was again used to draw curved lines one-half inch apart in the sections between star points, and diagonal lines were drawn at the ends of each pair of curved sections to make the feathers.

Before cutting the paper drawing apart, I labeled all the pieces and drew registration marks across all the lines to later help in matching seams. I pinned the paper pattern to my design wall and cut just one piece at a time to use for a template. I then ironed the templates on the wrong side of the fabric, cut the fabric pieces with an added ¼-inch seam allowance all around, and pinned the pieces back in place on the design wall. The sections between star points were used as foundations for paper piecing bias strips to form curves.

CHALLENGES OF NOT PLANNING

Sometimes a technique has to be invented to make a design idea work. I wanted to use strips cut from a chevron-patterned ikat skirt to encircle the central star. I had never done anything like that before, but because ikat is quite loosely woven, it seemed possible that it might work. I calculated the circumference of the new circle, then cut strips from the skirt and spliced them together. It was just luck that the final seam also connected to complete a chevron. I ran a basting stitch along the inner edge of the circle and pulled the thread,

easing the inner measurement to fit the edge of the pieced star. This edge was sandwiched between the central star and the dark olive background where it was caught in that seam.

One of the problems of not planning ahead is running out of a particular fabric. I've learned that, when tackled creatively, "not enough" can often turn into a wonderful design element. That was the case for the V-shaped inserts in the middle of each side of my quilt. There was only a small amount of one of the fabrics for bordering the center square. The strips weren't long enough to reach the corners, so they were centered on the sides of the square. After a bit of doodling, I decided to set in V-shaped pieces to cover the ends of the too-short strips.

My initial plan was to set the center star on point and fill the corners with half stars. I drafted one full-sized corner with half a Feathered Star and pinned it in place next to the completed center on my design wall. It looked terrible! The busy corner overwhelmed the central medallion. What to do? My husband suggested surrounding the entire center with more thin curves, creating a much larger circle. A small sketch incorporating that idea showed me that I could add a woven-looking pattern on top of the curves by inserting strips in the curved seams.

Detail from NATIVE WEAVINGS: FEATHERED STAR

Barbara Oliver Hartman

Flower Mound, Texas

I am fortunate to have a family that completely supports what I do, as well as many friends gained through quilt-making. Life is good.

MEET THE QUILTER

I began quiltmaking more than twenty years ago, but have been sewing nearly my whole life. My mother was a dressmaker and seamstress, so sewing was an important part of our household. Although my mother was never interested in making quilts when I was young, I was fascinated that my grandmother made quilts all the time and quiltmaking was an important part of her life. It was also a necessity, because recycled clothing and fabric for quilts were needed to warm her family.

While growing up, I had beautiful clothes that my mother made, but I did not fully appreciate her efforts because I liked the idea of store-bought clothes. What I wore never looked homemade, and my mother made sure that everything she did had a professional look.

Some of our greatest family battles revolved around my mother's making me sew. She owned a dressmaking company that made Southwestern-style dresses for retail stores and she had a number of women who did sewing for her. Mom was determined that I would follow in her footsteps and of course, as a teenager, I wanted no part of it. It was impossible to avoid completely, but sewing was not a burning desire I had.

When I had children of my own, I sewed for them from time to time and made curtains and other household items. I've always had a sewing machine, but it was not used on a regular basis.

Over the years I tried other crafts such as knitting, papier-mâché, and embroidery, but I never stuck with them for long. I sold real

Feathery Star

74" x 74"

estate in the early 1980s and spent a lot of time working in model homes. It was then that I decided to start a quilt. That was the beginning and I have never looked back.

It was amazing how much stored knowledge I had about sewing and fabrics from childhood. I remembered bits and pieces that my grandmother told me about the quilting process, but mostly I had to learn by trial and error.

Now, quiltmaking has taken over my life. I love to work on quilts every day and am irritated when interrupted by other things like cooking, cleaning, errands, etc. I have become such a one-dimensional being. It seems most of my activities revolve around the quilt world.

My family and friends, however, are the other things I do take time for in my life. My husband, Bob, and I have four children and six grandchildren. I am fortunate to have a family that completely supports what I do, as well as many friends gained through quiltmaking. Life is good.

Designing with Curves

This quilt started as an exercise in curved piecing with a foundation method and my determination to use two particular fabrics together in a quilt.

I have occasionally made quilts for the MAQS contest because it caused me to step out of my comfort zone and think in different ways. I did not plan on entering the contest this year, however, I had played with some Feathered Star designs and had some ideas for designs that did not come together the way I had envisioned.

A couple of years ago, I made a quilt containing this basic star design, but the star had straight lines (Figure 1). I played with one of my computer programs and put a spin on the star, making all the lines curved. I liked the design and began quilt construction. When about half the sections were complete, I attempted to put them together but it would not work because the spin

was too extreme. Back to the drawing board with new determination, I revised the curve on the computer and this time it worked (Figure 2).

Fig. 1. *Original star*

Fig. 2. *Curved star*

Once a pleasing design is accomplished on the computer, I print it on 8½-by-11 inch paper. Because it is necessary to have a full-sized pattern when using foundation methods, I go to a copy center and enlarge the design to the desired size. Going to print centers that have the large-format printers is handy, but it can be expensive if you do a lot of playing, so I like to give myself several options before I enlarge designs. If I am working on a design that is too large for the copiers, then it must be cut in sections, printed in pieces, and taped together. On this quilt, only the center was enlarged so it could be done in one step (Figure 3, page 15).

The piecing was accomplished with a lightweight muslin as the foundation, which gave the advantage of more precise piecing. The fabric base was easier to work with on curves than paper or other foundation materials, and it did not have to be removed. Sometimes, I cut away the cloth foundation if I am going to hand quilt or want to remove some of the bulk. Otherwise, it stays in the quilt.

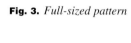

Fig. 3. *Full-sized pattern*

I liked the idea of the center medallion and wanted the rest of the quilt to have an irregular feel, so other design elements outside the central star were added and the quilt grew. While I was working on the quilt and nearing completion, the idea of the FEATHERY STAR started to emerge. By the time the quilt was finished, it seemed as if it had been made for the contest all along.

When the quilt top was complete, a simple design was machine quilted. The background was quilted by following the butterfly motif in the batik fabric. It was a lot of fun to do, but time consuming.

E-mail address for Barbara Hartman: winerunner@aol.com

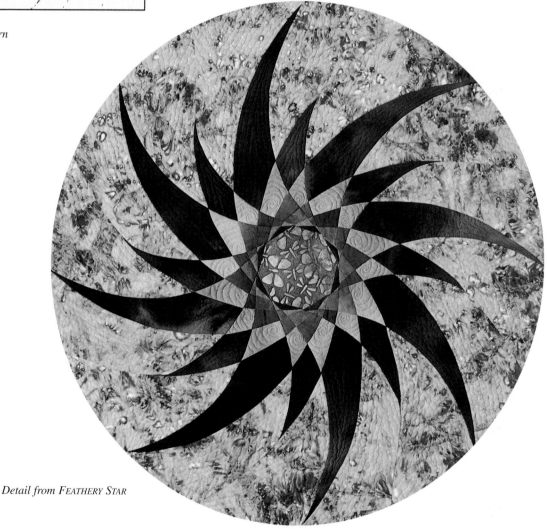

Detail from FEATHERY STAR

Nancy Lambert

Pittsburgh, Pennsylvania

Inspired mostly by nature, I am an avid gardener and look to my surroundings for inspiration on color and pattern.

MEET THE QUILTER

Inspired by a beautiful appliqué quilt many years ago, I became interested in quilting and thought I'd like to make something similar to that quilt. I had sewn clothes for many years, but had never made quilts. My quiltmaking began with traditional designs and has since moved on to more contemporary and innovative one-of-a-kind designs.

Quilting to me is a way to combine color and design. I like to work with a variety of patterns and expand them into a unique design. Sketching out variations, I spend a lot of time on the design of a quilt.

Inspired mostly by nature, I am an avid gardener and look to my surroundings for inspiration on color and pattern. I study flowers and all the colors that make up any one flower, then try to use them together in a quilt.

I try to fit some quiltmaking in almost every day. This may be just thinking about a design change for a pattern or sketching out an idea. I have turned a spare bedroom into my quilting room and keep my sewing machine and ironing board up all the time. There is a design wall covered with felt on which I can try various colors and shapes, seeing how they look from a distance. Many of the walls in my house are covered with finished quilts.

Mediterranean Blues

72" x 72"

I have always admired the traditional Feathered Star pattern because of the fine details of the feathers and the large impact of the star. When I first started to design this quilt, I worked on a curved design for several months. The straight edges of the star were made circular and the smaller points were added to this. I also worked on an overall curved piece.

For this quilt, I hand dyed much of the fabric. I chose a set of dye colors from Pro Chemical, including Cayman Island Green, Bubble Gum, Sky Blue, and others. I dyed 12-inch circles of each color, alternating colors over many yards of fabric. Techniques similar to hand painting the fabric were used with the dyes. Solid-color pieces of all the colors included on the main background fabric were dyed as well. This solid fabric was used for the appliqué pieces, in addition to Bali fabric I found for part of the background fabrics.

All of the stars were machine appliquéd. First, I rotary cut the star pieces, cutting quite a few colors and shapes. When most of the appliqué pieces were cut, I arranged them on the background. I used a light table and the star templates to arrange the colors and shapes. I arranged several stars at once, then fused them to the background fabric with double-sided fusible interfacing.

Once I had most of the stars fused to the background, I began appliquéing. A wide variety of metallic threads were used, as I varied the colors and widths to suit the star itself. This was the first time I used metallic thread for all the appliqué and found it to be a challenge in the beginning. I tried several needles and liked the metallic needles best. I found that adding a few drops of sewing machine oil to the spool of the metallic thread helped. Sewing slower than usual to keep the thread from breaking or splitting helped as well.

I plan to make several more quilts of this type and would like to explore other color schemes such as a more solid-colored background fabric. More machine appliqué could add dimension, as well as machine quilting more of the background stars.

Designing MEDITERRANEAN BLUES

To design all the star patterns used in the quilt, I started out by extending the main triangle, stretching it into a long, narrow point. I then drew the "feathers." At first, all the feather triangles were the same size (Figure 1), then I varied the widths and colors as they moved along the edge of the narrow point (Figure 2).

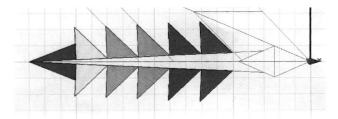

Fig. 1. *Original star point with feathers*

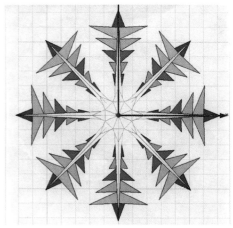

Fig. 2. *Two of Nancy's drawings for* MEDITERRANEAN BLUES

I pieced all the stars as units and appliquéd them to hexagonal shaped backgrounds, then added triangular corner sections to make the hexagons into squares. I ended up with squares that were 18 inches and 13½ inches. Once I had all the hexagons made, I place them on my fabric wall and tried a variety of arrangements (Figure 3).

I then added several 9-inch squares to the layout. Along the edges and corners of the quilt, I placed half or quarter stars and filled in the remaining background with strips that were 4½ inches wide by the appropriate length.

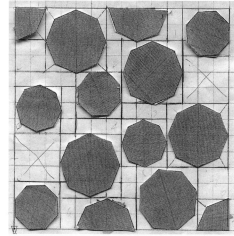

Fig. 3. *Paste-up of the final hexagon arrangement*

MEDITERRANEAN STAR Pattern by Nancy Lambert
This pattern will produce a 14-inch star. For an 18-inch star, enlarge 128 percent.

Add seam allowances.

Vicky Lawrence

Overbrook, Kansas

I just can't wait until the next idea is pinned in fabric pieces on my design board, ready to become another quilt.

MEET THE QUILTER

Living on a farm, my husband, Dennis, and I have horses, angora goats, angora rabbits, sheep, cats, and dogs. I enjoy spinning and weaving, but in recent years, this interest has been overshadowed by my interest in quilting.

I own a longarm quilting machine and do custom quilting at the Overbrook Quilt Connection shop. The owners of the shop encouraged me to make my own designs because I was continually changing the patterns on the shop samples. Their encouragement led me to start a pattern business.

I love making one-of-a-kind quilts such as the quilt for this contest. My husband is supportive and doesn't complain when supper is late or non-existent. He even helps me make decisions on which fabrics to use in a particular place. After looking at the design, he gives me his opinion and is usually right.

Support of family and friends has made this quilt and all the others made over the years possible. I just can't wait until the next idea is pinned in fabric pieces on my design board, ready to become another quilt.

55½" x 63"

A year ago, while standing in the large central room of the Museum of the American Quilter's Society, I saw an antique Feathered Star quilt in the next room. It had been pieced without sashing, so the star points touched. At that distance, the star took on a different perspective. Instead of the usual diamond shape that seems to exist between the joined points, the design had curved edges, creating almost an oval rather than a diamond shape.

That particular Feathered Star reminded me of a Venus's-flytrap. It had curved sides and teeth that trapped the unsuspecting insect which was drawn to its tantalizing interior. I smiled about the change in shape and filed that information in the back of my mind.

I pointed out the optical illusion to one of my friends, who said she had always wanted to make a Feathered Star but just hadn't done it yet. As luck would have it, the theme for the next MAQS contest was the Feathered Star. We needled each to get started on the quilts and to finish them in time for the deadline. We both were busy, so we might not have finished if we hadn't kept urging each other on.

To create the Venus's-flytrap, I drew the flower and leaf arrangement on graph paper, then went to a copy store in Lawrence to enlarge the drawing to a full-sized pattern. Wanting the flowers to be made of intense, bright colors, I browsed through a nearby fabric shop to see what could be found. After choosing several brights, I explained to the store owner my idea for a Venus's-flytrap that would be a regular flower shape with twisted petals, kind of like the plant in the movie, *Little Shop of Horrors*. She said that was one of her favorites, then smiled, and in a gravely voice said, "Feed me."

After shopping in Lawrence, I went to the fabric shop in Overbrook. I told one of the owners there about my design. She smiled, and in a deep, gravely voice said,

"Feed me." I was convinced then that the name for this quilt should be FEED ME.

Even after gathering several brightly colored fabrics, I just couldn't get quite all the shades needed for the flowers. Three friends and I took a road trip to do a shop hop. I gathered more fabrics on this trip to complete my wallhanging.

Without the help of my friends to get the right fabrics, find the great name, and get the project completed, this quilt would probably only be a thought in the back of my mind.

Taming Flowers

I knew that piecing the twisted Feathered Star into the pieced background would be a nightmare. So, early in the planning, I decided to appliqué the leaves and the flowers as units onto the pieced background.

In a class with Ruth McDowell, I learned to draw a full-sized master pattern and number the pieces. The master pattern is then traced on the shiny side of a piece of freezer paper, and the numbers are transferred to the freezer-paper pattern. Hash marks, made with different colored pencils, are added to the freezer paper to help match the seams when joining fabric pieces. In the class, I had made a wallhanging with straight seams. For FEED ME, however, I needed curved seams, and Ruth's technique provided the only sane way to go.

The whole quilt arrangement was drawn on graph paper, using four ¼-inch squares to represent a 4-inch square of the finished quilt (Figure 1, page 23). Then, at a copy center, the drawing was enlarged 400 percent, making the ¼-inch squares into 1-inch squares. I then proceeded as we had been taught in class.

The background was pieced by referring to the full-sized layout. I didn't want just plain squares, so half-square triangles were added at random throughout the background. The diagonal seams of the half-squares were arranged so that, on both sides of the flowers, the diagonal seams ran upward and outward.

More pieces were added to the leaves and flowers as the project progressed. In the beginning, the leaves were to be made from one piece of fabric, but something more was needed to attract the viewer to the flowers. So, on the freezer-paper pattern, I added an eye and a cut-out resembling a mouth to each leaf.

For the leaves, I traced the outline on the paper side of the freezer paper, so the seam allowance could be turned under and ironed to the shiny side, to which it would adhere. I then used a sewing machine to piece the leaves on the foundation. The leaves were positioned on the background by matching the pieced squares to the squares on the layout. (The squares were numbered down one side of the layout, then corresponding numbers were put on small pieces of fabric and tacked to the pieced background squares.)

The borders were not added to the pieced background before the quilt was appliquéd for two reasons. First, I wanted the numbers on the background squares to be as easy to read as possible until all the appliqué pieces had been placed and sewn. Second, I wanted to wait to pick out the border fabrics to see what the quilt needed; so the leaf tips on each side of the quilt were left unappliquéd until after the borders were sewn onto the quilt.

The flowers were drawn on the shiny side of the freezer paper. All the hash marks and numbers were added to the pattern. Cutting a whole flower apart at once would have created a mind-boggling jigsaw puzzle, so each freezer-paper flower was cut apart on the lines one section at a time as it was sewn. The pattern pieces were then ironed to the wrong side of the fabrics, and the fabric pieces were cut out with an added ¼-inch allowance beyond the edge of the freezer paper.

I matched the edge of the freezer paper on one piece to the edge of the freezer paper on the adjacent piece, pinned them in place, then sewed along the edge of the freezer paper. On some of the pieces with a curved seam, the freezer paper had to be released and the seam allowance clipped to provide enough give in the fabric to make the curve. After a whole flower was finished, it was hand appliquéd to the background.

As the quilt progressed, I began adding more and more pieces to each flower to provide more interest. After counting the pieces in one of the flowers, which was in the hundreds, I decided I didn't want to know how many there were. It was too discouraging. Beads were added to the eyes in the leaves and the centers of the flowers after the layers were quilted.

E-mail address for Vicky Lawrence: vlawrence@sftnet.org

Fig. 1. *Vicky's original drawing*

Maggie Ball

Bainbridge Island, Washington

Photo by Mark Frey

I'm fortunate to receive encouragement and support for my work from those in the quilting industry who are enthusiastic about teaching the next generation.

MEET THE QUILTER

A native of Northumberland, England, I am technically a barbarian because I was born north of the Roman Wall. In 1983, I moved to the United States with my husband, Nigel, and in 1996, we became resident aliens and are now here to stay. Living in Fayetteville, Arkansas, I discovered the beauty of quilts and was thrilled to see them displayed on clotheslines outside farmhouses.

I began quilting in 1986 and hand pieced thirty-six LeMoyne Star blocks during my first year, but had no idea what to do next. Fortunately, QUILT, the Northwest Arkansas quilt group, took me under its wing, educated, and mothered me. Sharing the endless design possibilities and the joys of a common interest with other enthusiasts was exciting.

We moved to Little Rock, Arkansas, and in 1992, I became president of the Arkansas Quilters' Guild. This group includes several exceptionally talented quilters, whose innovative approaches to traditional and contemporary quilting are inspiring and influential. They taught me much and I admire their work.

Since 1993, we have lived on Bainbridge Island, in the Pacific Northwest, an area rich in quilters and quilt stores. I volunteered at my son's elementary school and got more than I bargained for when a friend and I made quilts with twenty classes as a fundraiser. The techniques, ranging from drawing and painting on fabric to hand sewing, were appropriate for the age and skill levels of the children. The enthusiasm and creativity of the kids was a delight to behold, and the $10,000 we made on the quilt auction was icing on the cake.

Celestial Garden

84" x 84"

My continuing work with children has resulted in the publication of my books *Creative Quilting with Kids* and *Patchwork and Quilting with Kids* (both by Krause Publications, 2001 and 2003). Quilting with kids, girls and boys, is great fun, and they love it. Their energy and uninhibited approach is exciting and refreshing. Quilting with your children and grandchildren, or volunteering in the community, is a great experience. Ask your quilt guild to display children's quilts at its shows and to become involved at local schools. Your efforts will be richly rewarded and much appreciated.

I'm fortunate to receive encouragement and support for my work from members of the quilting industry who are enthusiastic about teaching the next generation. I recently became a consultant with David Textiles Inc. to produce lines of fabric that appeal to young, and young-at-heart, quilters. I love to teach quilting to all ages, enjoy making art quilts, and have had my quilts exhibited both nationally and internationally. I am a trained and certified quilt show judge through the Northern California Quilt Council.

My quilting partner for CELESTIAL GARDEN was Wanda Rains, who has had a longarm quilting machine since 1997. We've been friends for years, and ever since Wanda began her business, she has been custom quilting my challenging quilts. She always does a terrific job and we enjoy collaborating.

INSPIRATION AND DESIGN

CELESTIAL GARDEN evolved over a period of about eight months. It began with a wallhanging in mind, to be made from four or five Feathered Star blocks. I teach a Block-of-the-Month class to a small group of women and we decided to tackle the Feathered Star together. I was just trying to stay one step ahead of my students, and after I started making the blocks, four or five were not enough. I've always been fond of these complex stars, and decided to make nine blocks for a larger quilt.

My color choice was made before I had decided to do a full-sized quilt. I had just finished a Double Wedding Ring quilt with pale buttery yellow as a background in combination with blues and greens and the William Morris floral print. I wanted to use similar fabrics, but had one yard of a recently purchased lush red fabric that was striking, so it was included. Fabrics with pansies, butterflies, and bees provided the centers of the radiant Feathered Stars, and leftover pieces from the other quilt provided fabric for the LeMoyne Feathered Stars. Then, of course, I had to go out and buy more fabric! There was no more of the red, so every scrap of it was used, and the original ideas on its placement in the borders were modified. The quilt looks great on my daughter's bed, where the blue bedroom walls make the colors look even more intense.

Marsha McCloskey's book, *Feathered Star Quilts* (That Patchwork Place, 1987), was my guide for drafting and constructing the Feathered Star blocks. I adapted the patterns, to minimize the number of templates, and foundation paper pieced all the feathers. I'm sold on this method when it comes to accurate piecing of small triangles, and I also used it for the Sawtooth strips in the corner sections.

The sashed center of the quilt top remained on my design wall for about six weeks while the large corner sections were designed. Inspiration was a long time coming until one morning when the sun shone through a stained-glass star in my studio window. There, reflected on the floor at my feet, was the pattern. I realized that it was an eight-pointed star that would complement my eight-pointed Feathered Stars and immediately drafted the pattern.

The general layout of the corner sections is similar to my quilt INDIAN SUMMER, made in 1998. That quilt is illustrated in Margaret Miller's book, *Smashing Sets* (C&T Publishing, 2000). Margaret's innovative ideas and creative approach to designing unique block settings have strongly influenced me. INDIAN SUMMER has Flying Geese in the corner diagonals, but has the same large triangles with Sawtooth edges and the skinny wedge-shaped pieces that give a circular illusion. I liked the way this design offset the central field of blocks and decided to replicate it in my Feathered Star quilt.

Machine quilting is enjoyable, but when quilts are larger than about 70" x 70", there's too much bulk to wrestle with, so my friend, Wanda, quilts them for me. She specializes in unique custom quilting, using garden motifs as her inspiration. This is just up my alley, because I, too, like to infuse my love of flowers and nature into quilts.

Wanda seems to enjoy the challenge of adding her touch to an unusual and complex quilt. I was thrilled with the quilt and appreciated the quality and originality of Wanda's work. This quilt is a keeper for me!

Making CELESTIAL GARDEN
USEFUL DESIGN PRINCIPLES

Basic design principles are useful for quilters, and at the risk of repeating what you already know, here is a review of some of the important ones. It is good to keep these in mind as you design quilts and endeavor to make quilts that not only have a powerful initial visual impact but also have finer points that warrant a closer look. Time spent attending to details, accuracy, and improving your skills is time well spent. Every aspect, from the artistic design to the technical execution, makes a valuable contribution to the quilt.

Color and value go hand in hand and are usually the first things we notice about a quilt. Color may be what originally attracts you to a particular quilt, but the variations in value, that is, the contrast between light and dark, are what define the composition. After going to quilt shows for about ten years and studying the quilts that I really liked, it finally dawned on me

that the color wheel theory really works! Now I'm beginning to think in terms of selecting complementary colors and auditioning a variety of colors from around the color wheel. When piecing together blocks made by children, I realized the importance of my choice of sashing fabrics to display the blocks. This holds true for any quilt. The sashing fabric may make or break the quilt, and if you want the blocks to stand out, you need to choose sashing that contrasts sufficiently with the blocks.

You also need to consider the scale and pattern of the fabric print. Using a variety of print sizes, from solids or monochromatic small prints to multicolored large prints, will enhance the visual texture of a quilt. Often one particular print, such as a stripe or a complementary color, can provide a lively spark or accent, which perks up all the other fabrics you have chosen. It is well worth spending time auditioning several fabric combinations before you make your final decision. I often lay out a few possibilities, and then I come back later to reconsider them. Sometimes it takes several days for me to decide, and usually I wait to decide on

Detail from CELESTIAL GARDEN

sashing and borders until the blocks or center field are complete. It can be difficult to go into a fabric store and buy all the fabric for a quilt at once. Most quilters expect to be able to do this, but invariably, my quilt evolves as it is constructed, and decisions about the fabrics and layout may be changed.

The relative sizes of the components of the quilt top are important. Sashing and borders should be proportioned so that they enhance and not detract from the focal point. However, they should provide some points of interest so that the eye moves around the entire quilt and is not attracted to just one area. Diagonal lines are helpful for providing movement and flow. Repetition in the borders of a variety of sizes of the geometric shapes that are in the blocks will add diversity and visual coherence to the design.

DESIGNING CELESTIAL GARDEN

One of the beauties of the Feathered Star is that the basic pattern includes an assortment of shapes and sizes. There are small triangular feathers, diamond tips, and large star arms. The octagonal center provides an opportunity to selectively cut a motif, or it may be subdivided, as in the center block of my quilt. There were plenty of shapes and patterns for me to replicate in the four corners around the Feathered Star blocks. The eight stars, two in each corner diagonal area, are eight-pointed, like the Feathered Stars, but are smaller in size. The small LeMoyne stars with triangles are the same pattern as the middle of the center Feathered Star, but again, they are slightly smaller. The Sawtooth border mirrors the feathers, but the triangles are larger. The long, skinny wedge-shaped border pieces create a circular illusion. This border helps to link the four corners and adds to the impact of the design. Fabrics from the Feathered Stars were repeated, as well as the shapes.

Selective cutting adds interest and creates kaleidoscopic patterns within the corner stars. I drew several sketches of possible designs for the corner sections, chose my favorite, and then made a full-sized drawing of one corner to draft the pattern pieces. I always draw the pattern the same size as the finished size of the quilt, then add the seam allowances to each individual part. First, I drew the diagonal parallel lines from the center out to the corners, enclosing the eight-pointed star blocks. The width of these areas was determined by the block size, which was 10 inches. I drafted the pattern for the stars from a stained-glass star window ornament, and the small LeMoyne star in the rectangular block between these pairs of stars was drawn to fit into the space. The large triangles were added next, and drawn with a long side of 14 inches so that their saw-toothed edge of 2-inch half-square triangles would fit exactly. I decided to include squares on point where the corner sections meet midway along the sides of the quilt. The squares add to the continuity between sections and reflect the corner sashing stones between the Feathered Star blocks in the center field. All that remained was to draw in the skinny wedges and the outer border.

PIECING CELESTIAL GARDEN

The challenge of drafting the pattern was enjoyable, and once it was done, the technical aspects of piecing got all my attention. Quilters have a tendency to stick to just one method of piecing for a quilt. There is no reason why the technical shortcomings of using only one piecing method should hamper progress. I try to select the technique that will give the most accurate results. CELESTIAL GARDEN includes quite a variety of techniques.

Most of the quilt was machine pieced, but where the pieces are small and fiddly, such as in the LeMoyne star in the middle of the central Feathered Star block, I drew round templates along the stitching lines and pieced by hand. Don't be too shocked, machine piecers – there is a time and a place for hand sewing! For the rectangular blocks with LeMoyne stars in the corner sections, I also drew round templates and did a combination of hand and machine piecing. I used templates for the stained-glass stars too, pinning carefully and machine sewing along the lines. The centers of these stars were hand appliquéd circles – a good idea, but these are probably the weakest part of the piecing in terms of accuracy, because the circles had to be stitched between all the skinny points and are not as smooth as they could be. (Don't look too closely!)

Wherever possible, I cut my fabric without templates, but odd-shaped pieces are much easier to piece accurately if the stitching line is marked. In the Feathered Stars, templates were used for the star arms and the octagonal centers. All the feathers and diamond tips, as well as the saw-toothed border, were foundation paper pieced. This is the most accurate way for me to make rows of triangles, and I've always preferred it to the bias triangle method. For the skinny wedge-shaped border pieces, freezer-paper templates with registration marks along the edge helped me match the pieces. The templates were ironed onto the wrong side of the fabric, and the fabric was cut with an approximate ¼-inch seam allowance, using a rotary cutter. With a fine lead pencil, the sewing lines were drawn on the fabric around the edge of the freezer paper and the registration marks were added. The freezer paper was peeled away, and the pieces pinned and machine sewn along the pencil lines. When you use this technique, don't forget that the freezer-paper template should be a reverse image of the actual template because you iron it onto the wrong side of the fabric. If you don't pay attention to this, your piece will be a mirror image of what you want. My corner design was symmetrical with a mirror image on each side of the diagonal with the stained-glass stars, so wedges were cut in both directions.

I enjoyed the design and the technical challenges confronting me in making CELESTIAL GARDEN. Experiment and create your own designs. If you can draw the geometric shapes on paper, you can find a way to construct them in fabric. It doesn't have to be complicated. One of the great aspects about quiltmaking is that you can make a traditional pattern, however simple, into a unique quilt simply by making your own choice of fabrics. As your confidence increases, you can combine different blocks, settings, and borders and generate your own patterns.

Maggie Ball Website: DragonflyQuilts.com
Wanda Rains Website: RainyDayQuilts.com

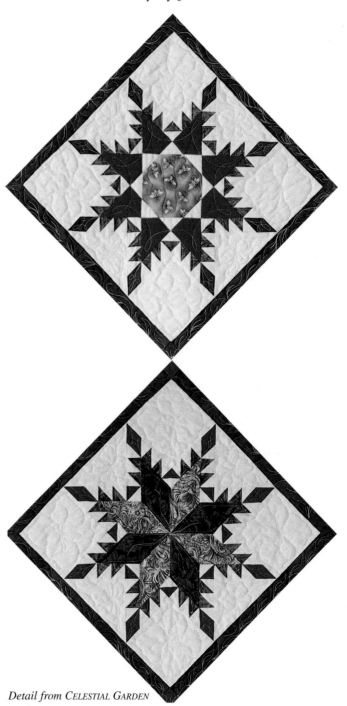

Detail from CELESTIAL GARDEN

Christine N. Brown

Castle, Colorado

I purchased fabric for my first quilt from a variety store, subscribed to the only monthly quilt magazine available at the time, and did not sew another garment for over twenty years.

MEET THE QUILTER

I am a sewing anomaly in my family. Neither of my grandmothers nor my mother was interested in sewing or quilts. My introduction to sewing came from my grandfather, who was the manager of a sewing machine store in Brooklyn, New York, for thirty years.

To demonstrate to potential purchasers how simple the machines were to operate, my grandfather encouraged me, starting at age twelve, to help him at his store. I sat at the window of his urban shop making aprons, Christmas stockings, and other items with brightly colored thread and decorative stitches. Not only did his sales increase, I discovered a love for creating things with fabric.

Through high school and college, I made most of my own clothes, including prom dresses and formals, as well as garments for my mother. Although it was a struggle to achieve perfect fit in garments, keeping at it for years improved my skill. Then in 1973, I saw a quilt magazine in a bookstore. Here was a new way to put my sewing skills to work, create a gorgeous heirloom quilt, and not have to worry about darts, waistbands, or fit. I purchased fabric for my first quilt from a variety store, subscribed to the only monthly quilt magazine available at the time, and did not sew another garment for over twenty years.

In 1985, a national quilt magazine published one of my original designs. This encouraged me to write about quilts and develop patterns, and I am still a frequent contributor to quilting magazines and other publications. My quiltmaking style alternates from traditional to non-traditional. Most of my quilts feature high-contrast color schemes and detailed, dramatic borders.

Feathered Dreams

59½" x 72"

In 1997, I was designated a certified judge by the National Quilting Association. This has afforded me opportunities to travel across America to judge both local and national shows, and conduct judging seminars for guilds and other groups. The most wonderful aspect of this job is the opportunity to see, touch, examine, and evaluate many hundreds of lovely quilts every year. Living in Colorado, I am inspired daily by a panoramic view of the front range of the Rocky Mountains, spectacular sunrises and sunsets, and sparkling night skies.

INSPIRATION AND DESIGN

In planning my quilts, I strive for unity and integration of the design elements, including block pattern, color scheme, sets, borders, quilting design, fabrics, thread color, finishing techniques, and all other artistic choices. Judging quilts professionally has given me a huge appreciation for the quilts in which each of these elements enhances the others to produce a beautifully integrated and well-designed piece of textile art.

My favorite quilts combine piecing and appliqué. I wanted a traditional look for the Feathered Stars, along with a dramatic, softly flowing appliqué border to contrast with the intricate piecing. When this project was begun three years ago, there were many Civil War-era reproduction fabrics in pink and brown, and these offered just the right feel for a traditional interpretation of this pattern. I also added fabrics from my stash, some of which were purchased over fifteen years ago.

Each of the 14-inch star blocks contains seventy-seven pieces and was machine pieced. Rotary-cutting techniques were used to make the small bias squares. Every other piece was hand cut and pencil-marked with a sewing line for accuracy. The centers of the stars were precision cut from a large floral fabric, which is repeated in some of the border leaves. Although the brown border background fabric looks similar in pattern to others in the quilt, it is actually a millennium fabric, imprinted with "2000."

The most fun I had in creating this quilt was choosing fabrics for the leaves in the border to achieve a harmonious gradation of color. There were many fabric auditions and dozens of extra appliquéd leaves made before the final arrangement struck me. I carefully measured for placement of the vines, but the leaves were positioned and sewn without measuring. The hand appliqué was done with a technique that involves starching the seam allowances and pressing them over a Mylar® template.

The hand quilting was done in brown and pink thread to add interest. The curved quilting design repeats shapes from the star center fabric for the open spaces in the blocks. Border quilting was done around each leaf and on both sides of the vine, with random leaf designs quilted in the open areas. For finishing the quilt, curved corners echoed the appliqué design perfectly.

Speedy Appliqué Preparation

This technique is fast, simple, and especially useful for preparing repeated leaf and petal shapes for hand or machine appliqué. I have tried needle turn, freezer paper on top and bottom, glue basting, and several other appliqué methods, but this one has the advantage of being easy and precise, and you don't have to cut away the background fabric after stitching unless you want to. By preparing all the motifs in advance, even large projects become easily portable.

You need a template material that is heat resistant, such as Mylar®. It is available from both Internet and mail-order quilting sources, as well as some local shops. Begin by drawing your leaf shape on the template material, then carefully and smoothly cut out your template. The more exact your original template, the better the final results. Remember that, if your leaf is not exactly symmetrical, you will have to flip the template over when you trace it on your fabric, to get the correct shape. If you make several copies of each template, you can work in batches.

Warning: It's important to use a template material that is made to be heated. Plastic template materials give off toxic fumes if heated.

Next, make up some starch solution. Boxed powdered starch is available in the supermarket for about a dollar and a half. You can follow the directions on the back of the box, reducing the amount you make if the project is small. Spray starch sprayed into a bowl can be used, but it makes the iron sticky and is far less economical than making your own. After each work session, put the leftover liquid starch in a clean container and refrigerate. Then, just heat some in a small glass dish in the microwave when you need it again.

Trace around your leaf template with a pencil on the wrong side of the fabric. I always position leaves, end to end, on the fabric bias, just because I think the seam allowances are easier to work with that way. Cut out the pieces, adding a ³⁄₁₆-inch seam allowance by eye as you go, and even narrower when approaching the points. No need to measure. You'll get better with practice, and it doesn't have to be exact. Heat a dry iron to medium. You can always increase the temperature, but the template will wrinkle if you set the iron too hot. I bought a small travel iron for nineteen dollars, and it's especially good for this technique because the tip of the soleplate is small and pointy. This iron is lightweight and easy to manipulate. To protect the ironing board cover, spread out several layers of old muslin, which can be washed and re-used.

At the ironing board, use a small, stiff paintbrush to dab a little starch solution on the seam allowances. Reposition the template inside the marked lines and press the moistened seam allowance toward the template. Try using a sweeping motion to get a clean, neat edge with smooth curves. Turn the edge all the way to the leaf point, then fold over the corner when you press the other side of the leaf. You can experiment with other ways to handle the points. The heat of the iron and the spray starch do all the work for you in creating crisp edges.

After finishing each leaf, let it cool completely, then gently remove the template and re-press the leaf. Position your leaves on the quilt top with a dab of washable fabric glue or with hand basting, and you're ready to sew.

E-mail address for Christine N. Brown: castlerocker@att.net

Detail from FEATHERED DREAMS

Jean Brueggenjohann

Columbia, Missouri

I love making art quilts as much as traditional quilts. They give me the freedom to add alternative media, such as paper, text type, and dyed silk.

MEET THE QUILTER

I became interested in quiltmaking in 1991 after taking an adult education class at the local high school in Granada Hills, California. The first block we made was a hand-pieced Nine-Patch. We also learned to make the same block by machine and received a worksheet of the block's variations. The next week, I brought back twelve finished blocks of variations. I loved this!

I took the class every semester until 1996, when I moved back to the Midwest. My teacher, Rita Streimer, taught me everything she knew about quiltmaking. A core group of us continued to take the class over and over, and we learned many techniques and skills. After five years, I felt ready to make anything I wanted. I can never thank Rita enough for all her help.

In 1994, the Northridge earthquake struck about five miles from my home. I was scheduled to go on sabbatical in the spring of 1995 from my job as a professor in the art department at California State University, Northridge. However, my plan to work making books was thwarted because the fine arts building was destroyed in the earthquake. I made art quilts at home instead, dyeing fabric and experimenting with embellishment. I love making art quilts as much as traditional quilts. They give me the freedom to add alternative media, such as paper, text type, and dyed silk. I still make these quilts, which are primarily shown in galleries. Since 1991, I have made nineteen traditional quilts and fifteen art quilts.

Rising Star

53" x 53"

My grandmother, Rosina Niemeyer Brueggenjohann, made beautiful quilts for everyday use, as well as special company quilts that were never used. My great-grandmother, Georgia Lee Potts Taylor, was a professional tailor who made men's suits. She also made beautiful quilts. I have a baby quilt she made for my mother, Georgia Lee Taylor Brueggenjohann, with embroidered blocks, flannel batting, and a cotton back. She quilted it on her sewing machine. My mom used that quilt for me and my brother, Dan, and I used it for my children, Carson and Hannah Reese.

I have been a professional graphic designer and university professor of art and graphic design for more than twenty years and am now an associate professor and chair of the art department at the University of Missouri. As a graphic designer, I love design that is precise, readable, and logical. Quilting is a perfect outlet for me. I like to think about a project, then put it out of my mind for a while and let my subconscious do the work.

I have always loved fabric. My mom taught me how to sew as a child. In traditional quiltmaking, I like for the unexpected or nontraditional fabric to make a statement with traditional patterns. RISING STAR is successful on that level.

I have recently been on research leave from the university and have done nothing but make art quilts. This time to work has been a great opportunity. I would like to make another traditional pieced and appliquéd quilt similar to RISING STAR. I continue to buy fabric that appeals to me with little thought as to what will be made with it.

INSPIRATION AND DESIGN
I started this quilt in 1997 after taking a Marsha McCloskey class sponsored by my quilt guild, The Booneslick Trail Quilters. I came home with a plastic bag of fabric pieces, which sat on my desk until a group of people from the class got together to make a finished piece from the class project. Everyone came to the first meeting with a finished Feathered Star. I came with my full plastic bag, a sketch pad, and graph paper.

After sketching out the Flying Geese and Sawtooth border, I had no idea how it might be used, but really liked it. I came to the next meeting with a finished Feathered Star; however, it was not the one in the quilt. The fabric was the same but in a different arrangement. I made a sample of the border, but once again, it was not the right fabric combination. I made several variations until reaching a combination that worked throughout the quilt.

I continued to attend the meetings and make more sketches. All of my favorite fabrics from my stash were chosen for the quilt. I love detail, and this quilt seemed to cry out for it with its precise piecing. I wanted to include ¼-inch borders and knew with the feathers in the star that the next series of borders needed to be simpler than the Flying Geese. I came up with the Tumbling Blocks for the borders, and opulent paisley fabric was chosen to be showcased in some way with a large border. The quilt just seemed to come together on its own, border by border, even though the design is somewhat complex.

The theme of the feathers is continued in the corner blocks. That theme flows from the center and is softened with appliqué, which was an idea that came near the end of the piecing. Without appliqué, the quilt was too abrupt and it needed something more organic like the shapes in the opulent border fabric.

The quilting design also came after the top was pieced. This quilt was difficult and challenging, and I loved each and every problem, delighting in the precision, fine detail, the flow, and the many facets of value. Each problem didn't stop me, but made an improvement in the quilt.

Preliminary Sketches

Very early, I learned to make an accurate ¼-inch seam allowance and cut accurately with a rotary cutter. As a result, precision piecing has never been difficult for me, and the more I worked on this quilt, the more the precise details delighted me.

I always make sketches for my quilts on tracing paper or, sometimes, graph paper. Usually, they are small, and I make as few as possible. This quilt was complex enough to require graph paper.

I made many sketches to work out value and contrast as well as to look at the scale of the different components. A series of sketches was made based on different quilting designs because I just couldn't visualize exactly how things would look, and the most important element for this quilt's success was going to be contrast and value.

Adding Appliqué

The design itself just seemed to evolve, and the fun lay in solving all of the design questions and problems. The appliqué was somewhat of an afterthought. The quilt needed more, and there was a geometric hardness and rigidity about it that needed to be softened. Also, a bit more contrasting bright color was needed. In terms of appliqué, I wanted something organic but still stylized and symmetrical. I thought about using my drawing ability for something more free-form, but that style didn't seem to go with the rest of the quilt. I decided that the stylized flower fit with the theme of the borders and picked up the floral print in the large dark borders. I really liked how the color in the appliqué moved from the center to the corners, and that brought about the idea of adding the red print quarter-inch border before the binding.

The appliqué was done with freezer paper and worked well even though the pieces were very small. The stems for the flowers were bias strips that were folded over and machine sewn to hide the seam.

Quilting Designs

The quilting designs are original, and were designed as the project progressed from the center out. The Celtic-inspired designs in the corners of the tan fabric were sketched, sized, and marked on freezer paper, which was ironed on the back of the fabric. I then used a light under glass to illuminate the design through the fabric, and traced it in pencil. The tan border quilting design was made following the Feathered Star, a variation on the Celtic knot design. There is a good deal of quilting in the ditch to highlight the design and some variation in the quilting that mirrors and enhances the design motifs in the borders. Most of the quilting in the dark areas is straight and mirrors triangular shapes. Again, variation is a theme throughout the quilt.

While I was in the middle of quilting the center of the Feathered Star, I took a class with Irma Gail Hatcher on how to improve quilting stitches. The difference it made in the quality of my quilting is significant. The single most important thing she said was, "You don't have to make multiple stitches. If you want small, close stitches, make them one at a time." Her advice worked. Soon I was able to make two and sometimes more stitches at one time. My quilting improved immensely, immediately. I spent many happy months quilting this quilt. It gave me the opportunity to relax and let my mind wander, because there was so much quilting to do. I loved every minute of it, even though there were many design problems to solve as the quilting progressed.

E-mail address for Jean Brueggenjohann: artjean@missouri.edu

Center star appliqué by Jean Brueggenjohann

Celtic quilting pattern by Jean Brueggenjohann

Barbara Clem

Dublin, Ohio

I first began to quilt out of necessity. Now I quilt because it is an expression of who I am.

MEET THE QUILTER

My admiration for quilts began in the early 1980s. Until that time, I have no recollection of having seen one, despite the fact that I grew up in a small town near an Ohio Amish community.

My mother and grandmother always sewed beautiful clothing. My sisters and I received sewing lessons by tradition because our grandmother taught our mother. At that time in our young lives we merely endured the lessons. It was much more fun to play house with our dolls. In retrospect, I am thankful that my mother persisted because these lessons became the wonderful foundation for my quilting.

At first, quilting was a necessity. Now I quilt because it is an expression of who I am. It is my creative outlet and something that is as much a part of me as my family. There are no sugarplums dancing around in my head, just quilts!

Fabric inspires me. It's funny how I can walk into a quilt shop and bolts of fabric seem to jump into my arms. Sometimes, a fabric will shout so loudly that I virtually begin that project right away, while others get added to my stash. The addition of a job, along with my family schedules, has made juggling time a norm for me. However, I try to budget time each and every day for me to relax and interface with my quilts. They add a special smile to my day. For the future, I plan to continue my pursuit of winning the big one in Paducah and becoming a certified judge and appraiser.

Circle of Friends

90" x 90"

INSPIRATION AND DESIGN

Feathered Star quilts have always been one of my favorite designs. I love the intricacy and accuracy involved in doing one well. CIRCLE OF FRIENDS is my second such quilt. My first one, MARINER'S COMPASS/FEATHERED STAR, had done well at many shows, but with our ever-changing art form, the traditional needed a bit of a twist to keep pace. With a recent long-distance move and my resulting melancholy spirits, I proceeded to pick out fabrics for my new quilt.

Color equates to sunshine, happiness, or a smile, but that was not how I felt at the time. In spite of the beautiful array of cotton fabrics I was seeing, CIRCLE OF FRIENDS would reflect more somber tones. Being without my inner circle of quilting friends after the move made me more determined to keep my nose to the grindstone.

While machine piecing my quilt, I still needed to find a way to express myself, adding that little bit of a flair that comes from within. When the quilt was laid out on my design wall, hand appliquéd flowers came to mind. The flowers were added as an expression of hope in finding new friends. I chose to hand embroider the buttonhole stitch with variegated floss around the edge of the flowers for added appeal.

When the top was ready to quilt, I spent days contemplating the design. I finally decided to sit down and work with the "known," thinking maybe the rest would come to me…something unique in a nontraditional manner. Hand quilting is my favorite part of a quilt. It's like the icing on a cake. Surface design is important and should always complement the quilt top. I began stitching and thinking, and thinking and stitching. Nine spools of quilting thread later, and many months, the quilt was complete.

The central quilted square surrounded by smaller square motifs reflected my growing circle of friends that I have come to know and enjoy since our move. CIRCLE OF FRIENDS turned into a happy quilt. It received a first-place award at the National Quilting Association show in Reno, Nevada, and has received numerous other awards at prestigious shows.

The thoughts of another Feathered Star quilt are still milling around in my mind. One of these days, an enhancement to CIRCLE OF FRIENDS may just pop out!

Planning Your Quilting Design

Quilting should not be an afterthought. Your quilting, hand or machine, should accent or enhance the piece. It is the difference between ordinary and extraordinary. When your quilt top is complete and ready to quilt, study it. Don't be in such a hurry to complete the project that you slight this very important aspect of your quilt. Ignore those seam lines and feel free to look at that quilt through new eyes to see endless possibilities.

Ask yourself…

1. What do you want to enhance or draw out in your quilt?

Keep in mind that outlining, sewing ¼ inch around the outside and/or inside a shape, will enhance the shape, just as solid fabrics and lighter values show off quilting better than prints and dark fabrics. Dense quilting, such as echoes, stippling, and small grids, creates the illusion of trapunto, when used in areas that are not so densely quilted otherwise. However, your quilting should cover the surface of the quilt uniformly edge to edge. The designs can vary within the piece, but large open areas with no quilting next to dense quilting causes distortion and "poochy" places.

2. Is this the best way your quilt can be presented?

Run though a couple of scenarios in your mind. Try to visualize the piece quilted. If all else fails, sit down and begin filling in the "knowns" and hope the rest falls in place, just as I did with CIRCLE OF FRIENDS.

Look at the quilting as the "final frontier." Feel free to explore to your heart's content, but most of all, enjoy yourself!

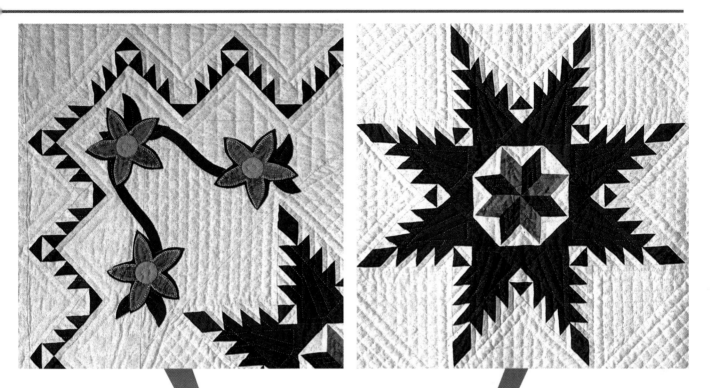

Details from CIRCLE OF FRIENDS

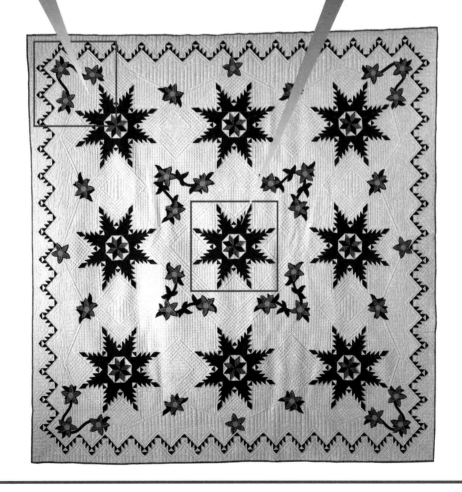

Gertrude Embree & Gayle Wallace

Shreveport, Louisiana   Taylor, Louisiana

I like the challenge of finding new combinations of colors to carry my message, evoke a mood, or express my feelings.

MEET THE QUILTERS

Gertrude Embree: My grandmother didn't make quilts, she went to garage sales. My mother was a high-kicking flapper who taught us to Charleston. A pair of Capri pants trimmed with black ball fringe was my first sewing project. Quiltmaking came later. First, I learned to sew and knit, weave, make baskets, and dye.

I love the instant magic of dyeing. My children remember hanging onto my heels as I hung over a cliff to collect lichens for natural dyeing. I made barrels full of Indigo vats for friends to gather around. After the yarn and fabric were dyed, we would throw our T-shirts, socks, and sneakers into the vat to turn them as blue as our fingers. Later, I researched the different classes of synthetic dyes and still use fiber reactive and occasionally disperse dyes. I taught all these skills after learning them.

One day, I pushed my weaving loom into the corner to make room for cutting out pieces for a child's quilt. Many years later, the Christmas stocking I was weaving is still on the loom because quiltmaking became my passion. I discovered design freedom. In weaving, although you can choose each thread you will use, many of the decisions must be made before beginning. If you make a mistake, unweaving is a disheartening process. I was hesitant to make unusual or original choices. For the quiltmaker, ripping out is a pain, but not a disaster. Unplanned additions or changes are easily accomplished and so, freedom to experiment, to step outside the mainstream and invent new approaches is easier.

Hallelujah!

57" x 82"

Being unencumbered by the traditions of quilt-making, I enjoy designing my own work and using whatever tools and materials are needed to help make the process interesting. I like the challenge of finding new combinations of colors to carry my message, evoke a mood, or express my feelings.

Gayle Wallace: I started quilting in 1985 on a lark. I took a beginner class at a local quilt shop and soon after was asked to teach in the same shop. Having sewn for the public for over twenty years, the sewing machine was my friend. I went from ⅝-inch to ¼-inch seams overnight and haven't looked back.

About ten years ago, I bought a long-arm quilting machine to quilt the sixty-five quilt tops that I had pieced for class samples. I'm still working on trying to finish those tops. Quilting has taken over my life, home, and studio. There is fabric in every nook and cranny.

There are so many people who have inspired my quilting that it would be difficult to name them all. When I started, there were few books available, and now, with the blossoming of new books on the market, it's hard not to want to make everything. For teaching, I like to adjust patterns to eliminate pattern pieces and make the designs easier to assemble. Quick and more precise assembly is what I look for in most of my classes, but when it comes to my own designs and piecing, the more patterns pieces the better.

Instead of fitting quilting into my life, I fit my life into my quilting. It has been a nice road to take, and the adventure has been a wonderful one. I've met some great people in the quilt world and taken classes from great teachers. The nice thing about quilting is that we can continue to grow with our skills and designs, and I hope to do just that.

INSPIRATION AND DESIGN

Gertrude Embree: The design for HALLELUJAH! came from my explorations with simple computer software. The final design expressed some of the wonder and joy I felt when watching a brilliant October night sky filled with shooting stars.

That evening, my daughter insisted I join her outside for sky viewing. The air was cold and sharp, and the scent of pine was underfoot and in the surrounding forest. The cloudless, clear black night was lit by masses of stars. It was another great moment in life, and I wanted to capture the memorable sharpness of cold and scent, the brilliance and energy of light against a huge darkness. The complexity of the design challenged me every step of the way. I had to transform the design from a small computer printout into a full-sized drawing and choose colors that would express the powerful feelings evoked by that night sky.

I have always liked orange; my orange crayon was usually worn down to a nub. Though not a favorite of most people, I don't care that orange is considered the ugly duckling of the color wheel. It has energy and power, and that's what was needed for this quilt. Were there doubts? Yes. During the lengthy and difficult construction period, I asked myself many times if those screaming colors could work.

I tried several ways to enlarge the design. A full-service copy shop helped me enlarge the 6-by-10-inch printout to a full-sized pattern on a blueprint machine. However, as the design was enlarged, so were the lines. They became nearly ½-inch wide. More problems with distortion occurred as the project grew larger. I scrapped that idea and decided to draw the design full size on two widths of a lightweight fabric with a preprinted 1-inch grid.

It took about a week to get the complicated design from the small printout to the enlarged grid, which was pinned to the design wall. To keep track, it helped to use colored pencils to roughly color the shapes as they were completed. Because mistakes are inevitable, it also helped to use a water-erasable pen for the preliminary drawing, then to finalize with a permanent ink pen. Before the design was complete, I deleted some parts of it to simplify construction. Then, I studied the design lines to decide where the paper patterns should begin and end and how to sew them together. The fabric grid stayed on the wall throughout construction, and sewn sections were pinned there when completed.

I needed to replicate the same full-sized paper pattern four to five times, so I made the first copy on graph paper, stacked that on printer paper, clipped the bundle together, and needle punched copies of the pattern with the sewing machine. I learned to label everything: each paper pattern piece, each color to be sewn on that pattern, etc. Because this was uncharted territory for me, there were many mistakes, and some days were spent ripping more than sewing. I learned to be methodical. I would rather, like Oprah, "fly by the seat of my panty hose," but that approach ended in screams and unmotherly language floating out of my studio windows. I had to be more like Hercule Poirot, and use method and order.

Friends and family would drop in to check on my progress. The white birch railing surrounding my studio space was festooned with possible fabric candidates, the floor was a mass of threads and paper scraps, and the collection of completed sections on the design wall was slow to grow. Most people went away shaking their heads. "It's that orange," I muttered to myself.

Month after month, I made more patterns, cut more fabric, sewed, swore, and ripped. As I stood about twenty feet away from the design wall, I began to see my original vision take shape. I even thought the huge scale was an improvement. As the dark smoky plum background fabric was sewn to the star parts, the colors began to integrate and sing, albeit loudly. This was no shrinking violet; this was the "Hallelujah Chorus"!

Computer-Aided Design

Gertrude Embree: I used to say that using the computer for quilt design is like using electric graph paper. I've discovered it is more than that. The design strategies that follow could all be done manually, but I doubt I would have thought of many of these approaches when I was using graph paper, pencil, and ruler. Drawing many of these designs would be such a long, tedious process that my mind would unconsciously rebel and reject thinking in that direction. With these new computer tools, the artist can move in unexplored territory, where she would always prefer to wander.

In 1984, I fell in love…with a machine. I was drawn to the computer by a demonstration of the new painting software. Eighteen years later, I have both learned to use paint (bit mapped) and draw (vector) software in my design work. You can computer draw any shape: a square, circle, arc, or line (straight or wavy); make it any size or any color, patterned or plain. You can move shapes around, group them, and duplicate a single shape or a group of shapes, infinitely. The "block model" of quiltmaking works well, and designing traditional quilts, based on a block or unit, which can be square, rectangular, triangular, octagonal, or any shape, with or without curves, is a piece of cake. The process is easy. New ideas are another matter.

One design strategy is to computer draw an enlargement of a traditional block then subdivide the parts into smaller, interesting shapes. The background can also be subdivided. Copies of this drawn design can be moved to the paint program, where it is easier to apply color to the new shapes. There you can go wild and try outrageous color combinations, subtle harmonies, visual textures, patterns, and especially, the effects of value contrast in various areas. When you go wrong, get another copy for more exploration (Figure 1).

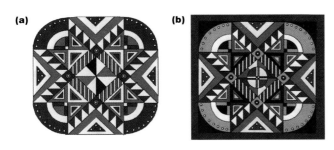

Fig. 1. (a) *Traditional Feathered Star block, enlarged and subdivided* **(b)** *Color variation*

Another idea involves deconstructing a traditional block into its parts. The parts may be rearranged, enlarged, skewed, duplicated, etc. (Figure 2). There are endless possibilities.

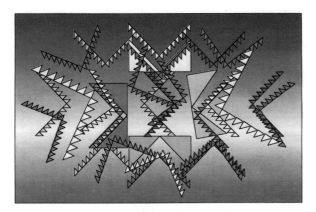

Fig. 2. *Feathered Star block deconstructed*

As soon as I levered myself out of the box that says you have to set blocks side by side or join them with sashing, original ideas flowed freely.

Using the drawing program, I discovered layering; that is, a block or unit can be made as a transparent line drawing, layered over another identical or similar block outline, and rotated to produce an interesting new design. Importing the layered design into a paint program enabled me to add color in the overlapping shapes (Figure 3).

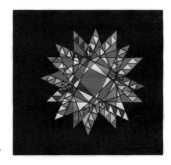

Fig. 3. *Layered Feathered Star*

I also discovered that some blocks are more interesting when color is added in the draw program before being duplicated and layered (Figure 4). Some exciting design possibilities resulted from this simple experiment.

Fig. 4. *The Feathered Star block was colored before duplication, rather than after.*

The basic Feathered Star design can be duplicated, colored, and the center square left transparent. When overlapped…Great! (Figure 5).

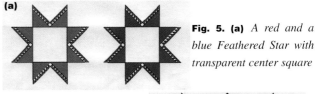

Fig. 5. (a) *A red and a blue Feathered Star with transparent center square*

b) *Stars overlapped*

But wait…Ta-Da! (Figure 6).

Fig. 6. *Overlapping red, blue, and green stars*

I love the simplicity and the "pow!" factor of this Feathered Star design. The area where the feathers appear to be white is actually transparent, which allows the colors of the underlying layers to show through. The colored areas are opaque; however, they can reflect transparency by blending overlapping colored areas.

The computer allows you to work rapidly in a series and to choose the best design to produce a quilt. In Figure 7, opaque white triangles were added to the single front star, and a set of black feathers was offset to float over the white ones.

Fig. 7. *Feathered Star overlapped seven times*

Overlapping and transparency can produce designs that would be extremely complicated to make if traditionally pieced. The one in Figure 8 would require another lifetime to sew!

Fig. 8. *Design complexity is limited only by your sewing skills and time to sew.*

My final design choice for HALLELUJAH! resulted from using these layering strategies and tweaking the results. The original star block had a hole in the center; however, that was removed because it would have been confusing for the viewer. Each duplication of the Feathered Star was moved a few steps horizontally and a few steps vertically. The resulting composition, with a long trail behind it, looked unlike any other quilt design, yet retained the graphic presence of the original block and added movement and energy to an otherwise static design (Figure 9).

Fig. 9. *Final design choice for* HALLELUJAH!

The process of design exploration takes time. I doodled around with the Feathered Star block for several months before I began drafting and constructing the MAQS quilt. I am still using pieces of the design and similar strategies to explore further possibilities for new work (Figure 10).

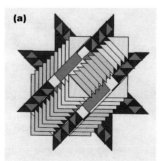
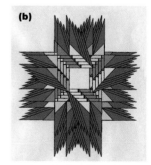

Fig. 10. (a) *USED STAR PARTS*   **(b)** *BEAR'S PAW PARTS II*

E-mail address for Gertrude Embree: gembree@sport.rr.com
E-mail address for Gayle Wallace: mgayle@prysm.net

Laura Fogg

Ukiah, California

I feel, smell, and hear my environment and want to express that in my quilts.

MEET THE QUILTER

I have been both a mural painter and a seamstress for many years. About five years ago, I began to combine my favorite aspects of the two media and go in a whole new direction…quilting. I had previously tried a few relatively traditional patchwork bed quilts but became bogged down in the process of making repetitious squares. Then I was lucky enough to experience two concurrent high points. The first was a two-week rafting trip through the Grand Canyon, and the other was a week-long collage quilting workshop with Natasha Kempers Cullen.

Coming out of a transforming experience in the canyon, I had to do art, and quickly found that a "painterly" collage style of quilting suited me perfectly. All of a sudden, I could create with fabric what I had never been able to achieve in any other medium. Landscapes became my primary focus, beginning with a series representing the immense and mystical beauty of the Grand Canyon and continuing with scenes that surround me at home.

Most of my life has been spent in rural northern California, where I have worked for the past thirty years teaching blind people how to get around with a white cane. Maybe it is this all-day focus on lack of sight that makes me treasure the visual world even more. I have developed a heightened awareness of my other senses and have learned to incorporate them into every action. I feel, smell, and hear my environment and want to express that in my quilts. I'm also irresistibly drawn to movement. To try to achieve a sense of movement in my pieces, I avoid the use of patterns, templates, fusible webbings, or basting. Everything in my landscapes is cut

Feathered Star Thistle

60" x 74"

freehand and allowed to move, twist, and flow as pieces are machine appliquéd onto the previous layers. I am fascinated by the inherent properties of fabric: its propensity to ravel, the fact that it has two sides with subtle color variations, and the existence of selvages that have their own totally different qualities from the yardage they border. I try to celebrate all of those characteristics in my work and work fast to achieve a more dynamic outcome.

My life as a quilter is indescribably enriched by my intense and wonderful relationship with a small group of quilting women in my community, the Mendocino Quilt Artists. We meet to eat, talk, laugh, and listen. Though we rarely work together on the same quilt, we work together emotionally to foster maximum creativity and artfulness in each of us. Each quilt is brought to the group in its various stages of completion and is open to the praise and suggestions from the dozen hearts gathered around. This process inspires and encourages me.

Other passions of mine are traveling, kayaking, mountain biking, backpacking, and organic gardening…all outdoors. These activities balance the solitary, sedentary quilting and writing. I actually contemplated quitting my job to devote full time to my art, but remembered that I thrive on diversity and changes of scene. So it's some of all of it for the time being, without enough hours in the crowded day to make a fraction of the quilts that keep germinating in my head.

INSPIRATION AND DESIGN

I started thinking about a quilt based on the Feathered Star pattern at the end of our long, dry summer. The northern California hills are parched in the daily cycle of cloudless days, and the sunlight reflects back to the viewer in tones of shimmering gold. Desiccated grasses, weeds, and thistles cling to life by their shriveled roots, waiting for the renewal of the first rain. In those dry thistles, I saw my Feathered Stars. The inspiration came to me instantly…a large star pattern in the sky

like a spirit, almost obliterated by heat waves, with a tumble of thistles in the foreground repeating the star pattern. To tie the sky and the thistles together there needed to be a landscape, which happened to be lying in front of me: the steep wooded road cut, the waterless ravine, and the collapsing fence line disappearing into the distance.

I wanted the whole piece to glow with the same light that was in the hills, so I pillaged my stash for silks, brocades, and other shimmery fabrics in shades related to gold. Most of the fabrics needed to be lightweight, even transparent, because there is so little substance to the landscape at this time of year when everything seems to float in the heat. Half of what I initially chose was discarded. The fabrics were too dark, too metallic in their goldness, or too flat. Only when I started cutting, could I literally feel what was right.

All of the work in this quilt is raw-edge machine appliqué, with the exception of the pieced Sawtooth border around the Feathered Star in the sky. The raw-edge technique suits me well because it gives me the freedom to "paint" with speed and energy. Nothing in nature is precise or symmetrical, and with this technique, I am able to cut, tear, and place all sizes and shapes of fabric with a total connection to the process of artistic expression. There are no middle steps or patterns to follow between the inspiration and the product. What I see is what I get, *now*, and if I don't like something, I can just move it, change it, or get rid of it, then put it back if I want to. The process is dynamic, interactive, and fast.

Capturing a Landscape

To me, it is extremely important to choose as subject matter a scene or place that has an intense emotional appeal, for it is the personal interpretation of a landscape that makes the work sing. I frequently work from photographs, but only those I have taken myself, and I prefer to have the visual image of the scene fresh in my mind, along with the smells, sounds, and sensations. A handful of flowers, weeds, or something else from the site set near my sewing machine at home, can remind me of the mood I want to capture.

The process begins with a piece of backing fabric laid right side down on a large table or drafting board. Over that is smoothed a piece of cotton batting the same size as the backing. The batting serves as a blank canvas, on which are arranged strips and pieces of fabric that form my collage landscape.

As in a painting, I start working from the background toward the foreground, which usually means starting with the sky. Though it is possible to go back and add details to the background after the rest of the piece has been completed, it is far easier to get the background finished before parts of it are covered by features in the foreground. Frequently, a sky may contain five, ten, or more different fabrics. The fabrics can be torn, cut into strips, shaped like clouds, woven like sun rays, or shredded and scattered in a playful wind. It is also fun to throw in odd bits of thread, yarn, or other embellishments to achieve a subtle sense of movement. That movement can also be suggested later by the quilting.

The important thing is to begin by covering large areas, overlapping the pieces by at least ½ inch to avoid their pulling apart during quilting, which would expose the batting. Subsequent layers contain smaller and smaller pieces of fabric and embellishments, but the underlying fabric layers are not completely covered.

In FEATHERED STAR THISTLE, a layer of transparent silk was placed over the sky and pinned through all the layers to hold it together while the project was quilted. Tulle or organza can be placed over the entire piece or over everything except the closest foreground details, both for ease of holding all the tiny pieces together during quilting and to achieve a particular atmospheric effect. In this piece, though, I did not want to dull the vibrant golds in the foreground and middle ground by

putting a piece of fabric over them, so I chose to skip the tulle and do the more difficult job of machine appliquéing directly over the raw edges of the cut pieces. The somewhat ragged effect was pleasing, because this piece was intended to look weedy.

The weeds needed to be exciting, dynamic, and detailed in their parched beauty to accentuate the sense of endlessly waiting for rain. I used fabrics, yarns, strings, threads, gold cords, and raffia to depict the weeds and thistles, which I had placed in a big Mason jar on my sewing machine table.

Plants are complex in structure, and there are dozens of intricate shadows and highlights that move all the time. I studied my weed bouquet and knew that I wanted a three-dimensional quality and a variety of textures and colors to achieve an impression of that complexity. Again, I worked from the back to the front, machine couching one layer of weeds over the previous one. All placement was random, and nothing was pinned. I just let the yarns and strings wander wherever they wanted to go as the sewing machine ran over them. The idea was to create a weedy hillside, not a cookie-cutter lawn.

The thistles, in their disheveled glory, were saved for last. The stems are scrunched silk, with satin machine stitched over the leaves for highlights, and stickers added with machine embroidery. The flowers are a combination of raw-edge stickers made of fabrics, and thistledown centers made of yarns, threads, and strings.

Parts were purposely left unsewn so they would move, change in the light, and pop off the surface of the quilt for a three-dimensional effect. The wide variety of materials, with different colors, textures, and reflective qualities, accentuates the impression of lightness and energy. The thistles are also disproportionately large to achieve a sense of immediacy and draw the viewer into the scene.

Bette Haddon

DeFuniak Springs, Florida

MEET THE QUILTER

I have loved quilts since my grandmother Gantz made me a Grandmother's Flower Garden as a wedding gift. I am self-taught in the basics of quilting but learned embroidery and sewing from my mother, Bee Bowman, when I was a child.

Quilting is my passion. It is my creative outlet, my comfort when I am troubled, and my interest-in-common with legions of wonderful, interesting, caring quilters. I love the diversity of the craft and appreciate all aspects of quilting.

I have a "golden moment" of precious time right now in my life. I have been fortunate enough to take an early retirement, made possible by my husband, Tom, and I have a healthy mother, children, and grandchildren. This gift of time allows me to spend eight or so hours a day in my studio, and I often hand quilt in the evening.

I set goals for myself and work toward achieving them. The worst that can happen, after all the time spent, is that I will have a completed quilt, even if it doesn't get accepted into a show or contest. In October 2001, I set a goal of having a quilt good enough to be displayed in the Museum of the American Quilter's Society in Paducah. In November 2002, I received the joyful letter announcing that my goal had been achieved!

I truly appreciate the quilters who have led the way in making quilts and promoting quilts to the status they hold today. I am proud to leave a small footprint on that road.

My advice is to dream, draw, do, and be persistent!

Star Shower II

88" x 88"

INSPIRATION AND DESIGN

STAR SHOWER II is an original design in which I was striving to incorporate the elements of color gradation, movement, and depth. The Feathered Star provides a strong focal point for the curved woven-ribbon effect sewn in vibrant colors.

My stash is full of cotton prints, and I sort them according to color, light to dark. I chose two or three different groups of green, blue, and bronze to add interest to the final piece. I also added grays to define the vibrant colors, calm them down, and give the eye a place to rest. Fabric selection is the messiest and most fun part of the quiltmaking process for me. After grouping the colors, I begin to cull fabrics that are too different, those that jump out of the light to dark gradation.

For me the joy of quiltmaking is in the doing. I'm a bit light on the planning stage; I like serendipity. If I knew how each detail of the final project would look, there would be no reason for me to attempt it. I really only "see" the quilt in its entirety when I'm photographing it for my records.

My skills have evolved for making STAR SHOWER II, with steady work since 1994. I was a true traditionalist in the late 1970s and early 1980s, and when I turned to full-time quilting, I wanted to try a new path. I love the curved, woven effect of this particular technique and plan to continue in this direction until it moves into something new and unknown.

Designing Quilts in Sections

I first sketch a design on letter-sized paper (Figure 1). The backs of nuisance mail are perfect for this. When the design is ready to make into a quilt, I draw it full-sized on white poster paper #18, which comes in a roll 36 inches x 50 yards, and pin it to my design wall. I then choose a color palette and mark my choices on each pattern piece with colored markers. I cut out one pattern piece and draw seam lines across it every half inch or so, to use as a foundation for string piecing fabric strips.

I used the following steps to sew each pattern piece:

1. Arrange each color family, of about seven or eight different fabrics, from light to dark.

2. Cut a 1½-inch strip from each fabric.

3. Place the lightest fabric strip in the center of the pattern piece, with the wrong side of the fabric against the back (undrawn side) of the pattern piece.

4. Place a strip of the next lightest fabric on both sides of the center strip and sew them to the foundation.

5. Continue adding fabric strips, building outward from the center, until the foundation is covered. If the last strip is under ½ inch, simply make the previous fabric strip wide enough to cover the end.

6. Place each completed pattern piece back on the design board, with the fabric *toward* the design board to check its placement, then sew the pieces together as each one is finished. The quilt will be a mirror image of the drawn pattern.

I free-hand machine quilt, starting from the center and working toward the outside edges. Using a different quilting design in each color segment adds visual interest. Masking tape provides a handy way to keep my stitches straight in the border area. Variegated thread was used on the top, and cotton thread in a similar color was used in the bobbin.

STAR SHOWER II is the best of my machine quilting to date. I guess each new work should be an improvement, and this piece really is a big step forward for me. I have entered the MAQS *New Quilts from an Old Favorite* contest many times, and this is my first acceptance. My advice is to dream, draw, do, and be persistent!

E-mail address for Bette Haddon: haddon@dfsi.net

Fig. 1. *Original sketch for* STAR SHOWER II

Details from STAR SHOWER II

Feathered Star: *New Quilts from an Old Favorite*

Agnete Kay

Calgary, Alberta, Canada

Computer designing would be slow and painful for me.

MEET THE QUILTER

It is hard to say exactly when my interest in quilting began because I have been doing many kinds of needlework since I was young. In the field of embroidery, I designed and sewed patterns for many years. Every now and then, I would see a quilt and think about trying quilting one day. Occasionally, I did make simple little checkerboard quilts. My interest in quilting really took off, however, when I attended a class in 1987. I haven't stopped since. The most exciting parts of quiltmaking for me are putting ideas to paper and picking fabrics.

I love quilt history, which fascinates me a great deal. The history of needlework provides quilters with a wealth of source material, which until the second half of the twentieth century, was not always fully appreciated. Books, such as *A Communion of the Spirits*, by Roland Freeman (Rutledge Hill Press, 1996), *Old Swedish Quilts*, by Asa Wettre (Interweave Press, 1996), and *Mississippi Quilts*, by Mary Elizabeth Johnson (University Press of Mississippi, 2001), represent my favorite kind of reading.

I enjoy competitions, too. It is nice to see your piece among others, to compare, to learn, and to enjoy. The many rejections to begin with were a little hard to take, but the acceptances were all the sweeter once they came. With not a little perseverance – more of that than talent – I eventually managed to get accepted in not only local quilt shows but prestigious international ones in America and Europe.

Mellow Moon

57" x 57"

Fortunately, I have been able to withdraw from the work force and find time to do a little writing alongside the sewing. (Not that life is less hectic when you become a grandma! Time always has a way of running a little faster than me.) In 1999, AQS published my book, *One Block = Many Quilts*, a wonderful event for me that has led to many other exciting things. I have met interesting people, seen interesting places, attended lectures and classes with wonderful teachers, seen quilts whose artistry equals fine art pieces, and found great friends around the world.

INSPIRATION AND DESIGN

MELLOW MOON began with several sketches. My first attempt at a Feathered Star looked nice on paper, but sewing it revealed some annoying disproportions. The second attempt did not go together as well as I had planned. The third time around, I achieved the hoped-for effect – something like a mellow moon coming out of an eclipse. While designing this quilt, I kept humming that line from *The Mikado*, "We're very wide awake, the moon and I."

The final fabric choices consisted of two chintzes, two regular prints, and a black batik-like shirt from the Salvation Army. Referring to my sketch, I made cardboard templates, scissor-cut the fabric pieces, and machine sewed the pieces together on the drawn lines.

For the border curves, I made a full-sized paper template half the length of one side, that is, from the middle to the corner. The paper template was the same width as the blue border strip.

For quilting the layers, I prefer simple patterns, such as chevrons or crosshatching. I needle-tracked (scratched) the pattern onto the quilt top. On some prints it was difficult to see the needle-tracked line, in which case, I resorted to a chalk pencil or tailor's chalk, which brushes off easily. I quilted the piece by hand in my signature style, which is a long stitch in perle cotton.

Designing in Stages

MELLOW MOON was designed in stages. In the first stage, I decided where the feathers would go (Figure 1).

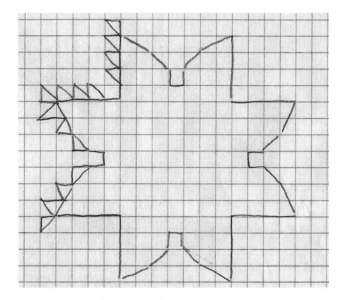

Fig. 1. *Original sketch of feather placement*

Then I experimented with design elements (Figure 2). As you can imagine, at this stage, it was by no means certain what would be dark or light.

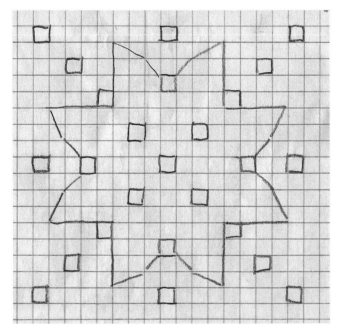

Fig. 2. *Added design elements*

In the third stage, all the pattern pieces and patches were placed (Figure 3).

Fig. 3. *Final placement sketch*

Sewing Set-in Seams

In MELLOW MOON, all the little squares were sewn with set-in seams. A set-in seam occurs where two pieces cannot be sewn together in one continuous line. Stated another way, a convex V-shaped piece is sewn into a concave V-shaped piece. If you cannot remember which is "vex" and which is "cave," just remember that a cave is hollow. Set-in seams are also known as Y-seams.

When sewing set-in seams, you must not sew into the seam allowances because the quilt won't lay flat if you do (Figure 4). Sew the first side of the V up to the intersection of the seam lines, then backstitch twice to lock your stitches. Cut the threads and remove the piece from the machine. Realign the pieces for sewing the second side of the V and, again, sew just to the seam intersections, not into the seam allowances. You can sew the sides of the V from the outside toward the corner, sew from the corner outward, or sew toward the corner on one side of the V and from the corner outward on the other side. I prefer to begin at the corner and sew both seams toward the outside edges.

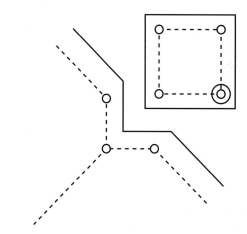

Fig. 4. *Example of a set-in square in MELLOW MOON. Sew just to the seam intersections (dots), not into the seam allowances.*

Detail from
MELLOW
MOON

Elizabeth Rymer

Hurricane Mills, Tennessee

Only by experimenting and trying do we succeed.

MEET THE QUILTER

Ideas for quilts are everywhere: color combinations, interesting shapes, fascinating textures. In a shallow basket in my studio, I keep a collection of interesting leaves. The colors and patterns in them make me think of watercolors. In another basket, there are some pretty rocks from the creek below our house.

I believe the Creator gives to each of us some creative ability. It is up to us to develop this gift. Only by experimenting and trying do we succeed. Of course, there will always be some projects that do not quite result in what we had in mind, but there will be those that do. Too many times, I think, we try to please a judge or someone else, but what really matters is what we think. If we believe our quilts are a feast for the eyes, then we have been successful.

INSPIRATION AND DESIGN

For the last five years, I have looked forward to the MAQS challenge. It enables me to look at an old pattern in a new way. Twenty-seven years ago, I began quilting traditional patterns, but through the years, I have turned to developing my own ideas.

Border Star

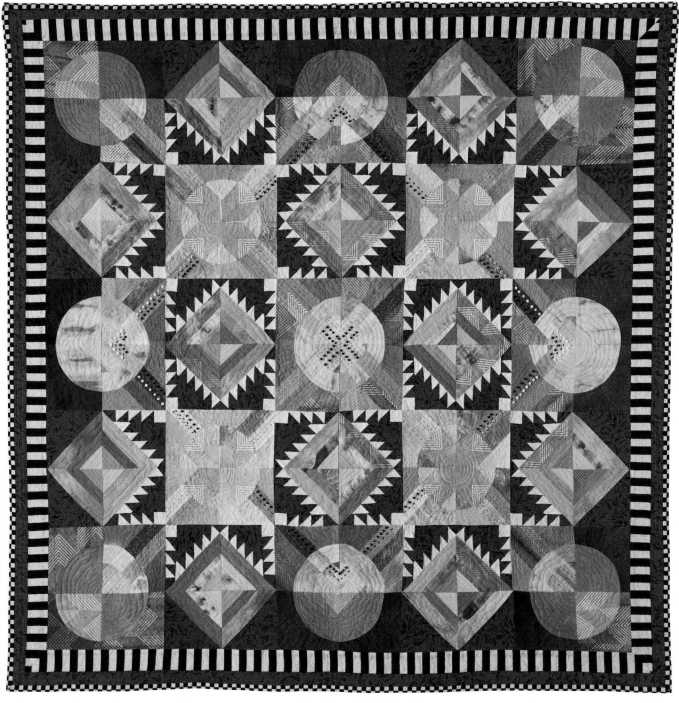

54½" x 54½"

It was well into summer before I began to think about the Feathered Star. Size was my first consideration. Many of my quilts have been quite large and therefore difficult to handle. I decided to keep this quilt close to the 50-inch minimum requirement of this contest. Using a 19-inch Feathered Star block resulted in squares and triangles large enough to be divided into segments for added interest and color. The basic idea from one of my earlier quilts, ECLIPSE I, provided the basis for BORDER STAR. It is interesting to create variations from one idea.

Several years ago, I purchased ten yards of white-on-white cotton fabric that had a diagonal pattern. I cut the fabric into smaller pieces and dyed them quite a few colors. This fabric, which has appeared in several of my quilts, gave me the star-like design in the center of some of the circles on this quilt (Figure 1).

To keep the Feathered Star pattern prominent, I decided to use a bright fuchsia in the stars, then began selecting additional colors. This may be my favorite part of quilting: adding and deleting color, stopping to dye other colors, and adding a few print fabrics to my selections…what fun! To bring out some of the diagonal lines in the quilt, I machine stitched in metallic thread and applied some beads and Heishi shells by hand, keeping these to a minimum so as to not overdo it.

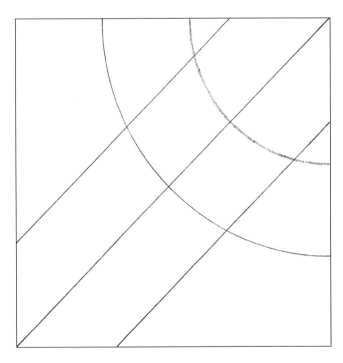

Fig. 1. *Drawings of circles used in BORDER STAR.*

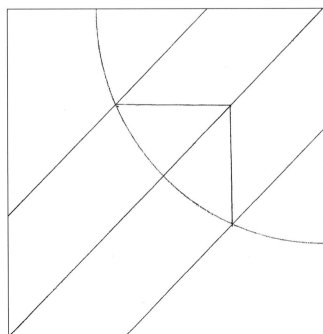

Feathered Star: *New Quilts from an Old Favorite*

Details from BORDER STAR

Feathered Star: *New Quilts from an Old Favorite*

Judy Sogn

Seattle, Washington

...I dream of being reincarnated as a great machine quilter.

MEET THE QUILTER

I started quilting in 1982 after years of clothing construction, knitting, and needlepoint. I have remained a quilter all these years because quilting offers such a great variety of techniques to choose from and so many different things to be made. I can make an ornament for a friend one day and start a bed-sized quilt the next. Appliqué may be the basis of my current work, but paper piecing waits for my next project. I can work at my sewing machine in the comfort of my sewing room or carry handwork with me on vacations or to my appointments. While some friends dread retirement and having nothing to do, I know there will always be some project on my to-do list, and if I were to reach the bottom of that list, there would be something new to inspire me just around the corner.

I am constantly inspired and challenged by the quilts of others. I enjoy designing original works but also like recreating a quilt I particularly admire. The joy is in the doing for me. I may try something only once, but finding out that I can do it is rewarding. I've also learned there are many things I can't do, and that makes me appreciate the work of others all the more. The green-eyed monster, jealousy, attacks me occasionally, and I dream of being reincarnated as a great machine quilter. Consequently, my dream for the future is an affordable, easy to use, easy to maintain machine somewhere between a conventional sewing machine and a longarm quilting machine.

Stars on Ice

52" x 52"

INSPIRATION AND DESIGN

When starting to work on an idea for the Feathered Star design, I looked at a computerized pattern source and found a block from 1934 that was interesting. I started manipulating and modifying this block until it became my own design. During this process, I accidentally produced a Feathered Star design that could be easily foundation paper pieced, my current favorite quilting technique. The original 1934 design was illustrated in blue, which reminded me of a snowflake, so I worked with a cool blue palette and kept visions of snow and ice dancing in my head. I am a big fan of ice skating, which led me to the title STARS ON ICE.

I found a beautiful quilted feather design in Barbara Chainey's *The Essential Quilter Project Book* (David & Charles, 1997) and adapted it for the plain squares. When one-fourth of the design was placed in the squares between the star points, the quilted feathers formed their own Feathered Star design, an unforeseen but happy coincidence. The border was the result of another happy accident. When it came time to plan the border, I was unsure of what to do, so I started playing with border options on the computer. I find that the computer allows me to explore intricate designs that would be nearly impossible to create with paper and pencil. One of the first designs was simple to piece even though it looked somewhat complicated. This border design led me to a different shape for the outside edges of the quilt.

My biggest challenge for STARS ON ICE was finding the proper values for the background and for the stars. I wanted to have three different values in the background, which made it challenging to find fabrics for the stars so they would stand out. I prefer multi-fabric quilts, both because they are more interesting to view and, more importantly, more interesting for me to make. Of course, this means more fabric to purchase, but that's a big part of the fun, too.

After finishing the quilt top, I found one more area for Feathered Stars – the quilt backing. A pieced Feathered Star would have contained far too many seams for the back of the quilt. Instead I chose four beautiful blue fabrics with printed feather designs. I placed these fabrics in four large, simple Nine-Patch stars, and thus my quilt has Feathered Stars times three.

Labels are another important part of my quilts. I enjoy designing my labels, using computer clip art and the wonderful fonts available to us now through quilting software. I found a beautiful clip art border with snow-flakes for the label that fits nicely with my icy theme.

Detail from STARS ON ICE

Foundation Pattern for One Star Point
by Judy Sogn

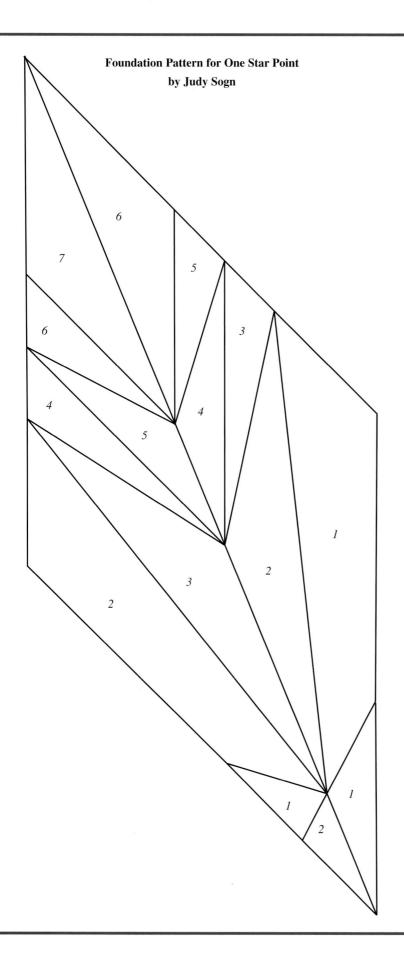

Detail of star point

Kristina Chase Strom

Glendale, Ohio

It was like making hundreds of little quilts!

MEET THE QUILTER

One of my first toys was a hand-quilted patchwork puppy, made by my Aunt Helen Chase. My mother often told the story that, when she washed "Patches" and hung her to dry on the clothesline outside the nursery window, I would stand in my crib and cry inconsolably. I sometimes think my attachment to that beloved cloth companion was the subliminal seed of my lifelong interest in quiltmaking, either that or a natural inclination toward rebellion!

Though my mother began teaching me most of the "womanly arts" – sewing, knitting, crochet, embroidery, needlepoint, beading, rug braiding, latching, hooking, weaving, knotting, and lacemaking – from the time I developed sufficient hand-eye coordination to feed myself, she touched only briefly on piecing and quilting. When, as a child, I asked her why, her answer was always the same: during the Great Depression, despite extreme hardship, she and the other women in her Boston family were never "reduced to patchwork." Still, she respected and supported my interest in the field. Many years later, shortly before she died, my mother pieced her first quilt top and expressed regret that she had allowed herself to be influenced by such a misinformed construct.

What quilting means to me and what inspires my work are inextricably intertwined. My involvement in this art form resonates deep inside of me. When I am working, I feel an almost primal connection not only with my own creative nature but also with that of quilters everywhere and throughout time.

Starred & Feathered

78" x 78"

At this point in time, I think there are some people who would ask me how I fit my life into my busy quilting. Seriously, though, creating the time and space to quilt had long been a challenge until recently. Now, my daughters are grown, and basically I have intentionally claimed a certain number of hours a week to quilt, time I formerly devoted to active mothering. When they visit and remark about how much I have accomplished, I reply, "Now you know how much energy I spent on you!"

My quilting ideas and dreams for the future are constantly evolving. Each project seems to have a life of its own, which guides me in unexpected, but always exciting, new directions. For now though, I see myself continuing to explore quilting history and incorporating it in my work. I also imagine I will eventually integrate my other lifelong passion, writing, with my quilting in some way.

INSPIRATION AND DESIGN

My vision in conceiving STARRED & FEATHERED was to construct the historical Feathered Star block by using a utilitarian, currently popular technique, thus marrying the magnificent with the mundane, the past with the present. I wanted to elevate the status of the common "raggy" quilt to a place I call "shaggy chic" and simultaneously bring a marvelous and intricate heirloom out of the "don't touch: save for posterity chest," all the while retaining design integrity. My hope was to create an elegant quilt that would actually be used as well as cherished.

For the center star medallion, as well as the partial stars, I enlarged and modified a foundation pieced pattern after first seeing this variation in Barbara Brackman's *Encyclopedia of Pieced Quilt Patterns* (American Quilter's Society, 1993). I created window templates by tracing the components separately on template plastic. After adding ½-inch seam allowances, I traced and cut 528 patches, each from

100-percent cotton fabrics, for the front and back, plus sashing and borders. I selectively cut the star points to feature two motifs and cut the hexagonal star centers for a kaleidoscopic effect. I chose backing fabrics that I thought would add a further dimension of color to the frayed edges.

Using window templates as guides for each unit, I cut out the required amount of fusible batting, slightly inside the line. I sandwiched and pressed each unit, machine stitched along the seam line, and machine quilted the bigger units. It was like making hundreds of little quilts! I assembled the mini-quilts right sides together, clipping every ⅛ inch along the seam allowance and inset areas as I went along. I constructed the star and partial stars individually and joined them with sashing, using a concealed sashing for the medallion. I made a mitered frame of two border fabrics and binding, which I then attached to the body. I attached a two-color sleeve for hanging so as to not detract from the design on the back. Taking a deep breath, I drove to the local laundromat where, after scouring out an industrial machine, I gently washed the quilt twice to enhance the shaggy effect before proceeding to the dryer.

The most challenging aspect of making this quilt was organizing all the various components before and during assembly. I ended up relying on two full-sized design walls, one in the living room and one in my sewing studio, along with a number of cardboard under-bed storage cartons and five layout diagrams to guide me. For a while, my family thought that every available space in our entire house was dedicated to this project, a sentiment not too far from the truth.

There are several things I like about STARRED & FEATHERED. The whimsical shaggy edges on the front make me smile. Graphically, I am pleased with the overall design, whether viewed close up or from a distance, which I believe showcases and enhances this lovely pattern in a deceptively simple way. Perhaps my favorite aspect of the quilt is the distinct design that serendipitously evolved on the back, making the quilt completely reversible, each side reflecting a different mood and interpretation – what a pleasant surprise!

As far as expanding on this design, while I was making the quilt, my mind whirled with ideas of how to fine tune this technique and apply it to other relatively complex traditional quilt blocks. Toward this end, I began keeping a notebook of sketches dedicated to shaggy chic quilts I plan to make.

Divide and Conquer

Whether making a quilt from an adaptation of a traditional block or creating an original design, I spend a considerable amount of time drafting, planning, and experimenting with ideas before starting the actual project. I have learned the hard way that rushing this phase more often than not leads to frustration and, occasionally, outright failure even when creating a relatively simple piece. STARRED & FEATHERED was no exception to this self-imposed rule.

After an image of this quilt had floated around in my imagination long enough to inspire me, I sketched rough layout designs and narrowed my options to two. Becoming more serious, I drew the blocks to scale. Choosing between the layouts, in this case, was simple. One in which the center block was set on point would have ended up being a minimum of 120 inches square. While I am used to wrestling with alligators on my home sewing machine, tackling a quilt this size would have pushed me beyond sanity.

Once my layout was finalized (Figure 1), my next step was what I call "divide and conquer." Because of space constraints and the limitations of my equipment, I make larger quilts in sections. There were three workable components in STARRED & FEATHERED, which were again drafted to scale (Figure 2).

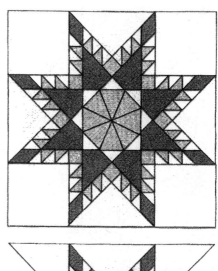

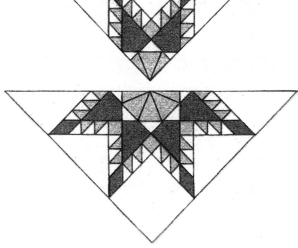

Fig. 1. *Final drawing of STARRED & FEATHERED*

Fig. 2. *Three workable components*

Next, I isolated the patches (Figure 3). Finally, I developed a construction strategy based on the drawings.

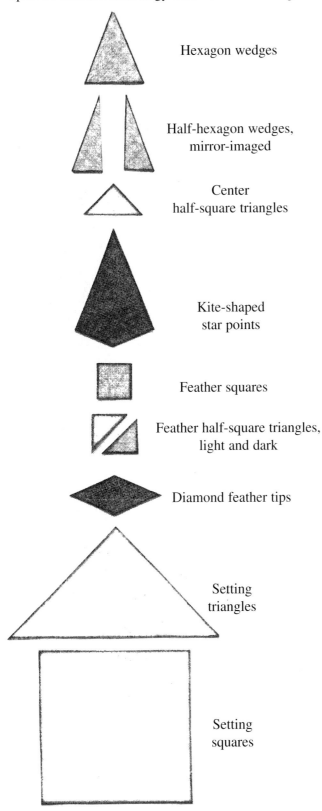

Hexagon wedges

Half-hexagon wedges, mirror-imaged

Center half-square triangles

Kite-shaped star points

Feather squares

Feather half-square triangles, light and dark

Diamond feather tips

Setting triangles

Setting squares

Fig. 3. *Patch shapes for* STARRED & FEATHERED

Because the Feathered Star block measured twenty inches finished and my design called for a 34-inch central motif, I took my drawing of the components to the printer for enlarging. The shop I frequent has a copier used for architectural drawings, which was perfect for this project. Though mathematically the size I needed for each of the components was 1.7 times the original, I have learned to fiddle with the settings until I get what I want, which in this case was somewhere in the range of 220–230 percent. Most importantly, experience has taught me to measure each individual patchwork unit in the enlarged copies before I leave. Nothing is worse than struggling with hundreds of half-square triangles with two sides that measure $2\frac{3}{8}$ inches finished. Referring to my drawing, I meticulously measured each segment with my quilting ruler, ignoring the quizzical stares of the other customers. In the case of STARRED & FEATHERED, I lucked out. All the units were in ½-inch increments.

Back at home, I played around with some scrap fabric and batting remnants to determine the most accurate and efficient way to assemble each component. I found out right away that, for the quilt to turn out as desired, a refined approach would be required, which was fine with me because I really enjoy intricate piecing. I ended up making plastic templates for each unit and adding a ½-inch allowance around all the patches, except for the seams of adjoining hexagonal wedges. I had to be especially mindful of the ½-inch allowance, because the automatic pilot in my quilter's brain is set to ¼ inch. These templates considerably streamlined the cutting, organizing, and preliminary assembling of the myriad pieces.

When at last I began to sew, I pinned the construction strategy guides to my studio design wall (Figure 4, page 75), as well as the overall layout (shown in Figure 1, page 73), which proved to be of enormous help in reducing confusion as to where each unit was placed and in what order sewn.

Feathered Star: *New Quilts from an Old Favorite*

Drafting and planning STARRED & FEATHERED was a challenging adventure, a process that, looking back, I enjoyed almost as much as making the quilt. As each component was completed and pieced together, I would stand back and look and get so excited. My design was working just as I had envisioned. Oh, what a feeling!

Detail from STARRED & FEATHERED

Fig. 4. *Construction guides* **(a)** *Center block* **(b)** *Side units* **(c)** *Corner units*

The back of STARRED & FEATHERED

Sue Turnquist

Harrisburg, Missouri

MEET THE QUILTER

Obsession. Addiction. Compulsion. These are words that immediately come to mind when someone asks how quilting affects my life. Quilting goes hand in hand with eating and breathing as an absolute necessity in my daily life. Everyone is innately creative, but not everyone is fortunate enough to discover his or her creative niche. I'm grateful to have discovered quilting and wish I could have done so much earlier in my life. There are so many quilts dancing in my head and so little time!

Quilting has not only taken over my life, as my husband can attest, it has taken over my house. I began my quilting career in a basement studio but moved upstairs when my husband started building custom fly rods as a hobby. Epoxy glue, cork dust, and fabric do not mix, although we do share a love of decorative threads. Now I occupy the dining room, living room, and one bedroom but hope to have a real studio and reclaim my house in the near future.

My full-time job as a veterinary pathologist leaves only a limited amount of time to devote to sewing. Dust bunnies frolic under my bed, and my idea of a hot dinner is a take-and-bake pizza. My husband is a good sport and recognizes my need to pursue my creative outlet. He also turns a blind eye to my quilt-related expenditures. He gallantly carries my fabric bolts on those occasions when he accompanies me to the fabric store, and for my birthday, he treats me to a fabric shopping spree.

I try to learn something from every quilt I make. This one taught me to listen to my heart and not a time schedule.

Shooting Stars & Ruffled Feathers

69" x 69"

Our home is quite secluded on a lake in the middle of a large wooded acreage. Deer, foxes, turkeys, and wild Canada geese raise their families in our yard, and the miracles that happen outside my window are a source of constant awe. Earlier this year, we watched a pair of fox kits chase grasshoppers, under the watchful eye of their mother. Because we live in this paradise, it is no surprise that many of my quilts reflect a nature theme. My work has taken a new turn this year with my interest in Log Cabin variations. Who knows where the next path will take me.

INSPIRATION AND DESIGN

Before the design for this quilt was conceived, I tossed around potential names. This is not how I generally work, but I am not overly fond of the Feathered Star block and hoped a catchy name would spur my interest. Focusing on the word "feather," I considered horse feathers, feather-brained, birds of a feather, feather your nest, and others. I finally settled on RUFFLED FEATHERS, envisioning a free form Feathered Star block. I am not much of a planner when it comes to quiltmaking. My quilts tend to evolve as the work progresses. I start with an idea for the predominant section and take it from there. I seldom have a vision of how the finished quilt will look before the work begins.

The design process began with a series of rough sketches of free form Feathered Star blocks alternating with one-quarter Log Cabin blocks. The final sketch was then transferred to a piece of paper from a sixty-inch wide roll. If only freezer paper were packaged in that size. The RUFFLED FEATHERS quilt was drawn on the paper free-hand. Registration marks were added to the seam lines to facilitate reassembling the blocks after piecing.

In the meantime, I had decided that my palette would include gradations of brown and blue fabrics. During all of this process, the "quilt-in-progress" and I had been having a dialogue. I frequently have conversations with my evolving quilts and usually try to listen to what they are saying. This particular quilt not only spoke to me, it screamed.

The dialogue went something like this:

Quilt: "Yeah, I like the design. Are you sure about this blue and brown color thing?"

Me: "Yeah, the design rocks. You'll like the colors. The color gradations are great!"

Quilt: "Brown and blue, huh?"

Me: "Yes. I've already pulled all these lovely browns and blues. Don't worry, it will work!"

At this point, every suitable brown and blue fabric from my stash has been pulled and ironed, and my rotary cutter is poised to make the first cut.

Quilt: "STOP!!! Where in the world is your head? What are you thinking? This is a happy quilt, and it wants to revel in vibrant, knock-your-socks-off colors!"

Me: "You think so?"

Quilt: "I know so! You go back into your stash and pull out all of those bright batiks you've been fondling for years, and don't stop until you've got them all!"

Me: "But I've just ironed all of the brown and blue fabric, and I've got a deadline to meet."

Quilt: "Trust me. Put it away. It'll still be good the next time you want to use it."

Thank goodness I listened to this advice. I returned to my stash and pulled out all of the yellow, orange, fuchsia, purple, lime green, blue, and teal batiks. Piecing and assembly was a joy. The fabrics exude happiness, and I eagerly anticipated every sewing session.

The setting corner triangles were designed after the center medallion was finished. Several designs were auditioned before the shooting chevrons were chosen. After the size was calculated, the triangles were cut out of white paper, and the design was drawn, again with added registration marks to aid in reassembly. The chevrons were paper-pieced.

I try to learn something from every quilt I make. This one taught me to listen to my heart and not a time schedule. It is definitely a happy quilt. I can't help but smile each time I see it.

E-mail address for Sue Turnquist: turnquists@missouri.edu

Details from SHOOTING STARS & RUFFLED FEATHERS

S. Cathryn Zeleny

Napa, California

The key to personal style is being consistent...

MEET THE QUILTER

I am a visual artist (acrylic and pencil) who discovered quilting a little over three years ago. At that time, I was struggling to find more personal meaning in my painting and to develop a cohesive style. Quilting provided a break from that frustrating, nebulous, and sometimes scary task. Using fabric as a medium, doing piecing and appliqué, and learning to free-motion quilt were mostly fun exercises in new techniques. A viable design idea from a fabric, a challenge, or a design problem would be turned into a quilt without concern for how it related to either my previous work or to my goals as an artist. I completed twenty-one art quilts of original design. Now, though, I have reached the same point where I was in painting. It is time to do the hard part, to create a body of work in quilting that is artistically mature and distinctly my own.

As I look back over my work of the past three years, I can see that many creative choices are working well. My quilts have elaborate piecing and contrasting appliqué. My fabrics are crisp-looking cottons of contemporary patterns that are mid-to-bright in intensity and have a good range of values. There is usually a concise theme portrayed as a single understandable image, and the inspirations for my quilts are usually design oriented, that is, either problems to be solved technically or disparate elements to

Stars of a Different Feather

54" x 72"

be placed in unusual ways. However, I have repeatedly made choices that are not successful. I place values in gradations that do not have enough contrast to make the shapes or patterns stand out well. Often my color choices are too limited, which results in a less dynamic image than I would like. While most of my quilts are visually interesting and unique in idea, they generally do not have an emotive message or personal meaning beyond the design. I still tend to fix compositional problems with the first solution I think of rather than seeking a better alternative.

My goal, then, for the coming years of quiltmaking, is to address the issues of personal style and to create a cohesive body of work. I intend to build on the foundation of my successful choices and on the techniques that have proven sound. By working in a series, I hope to establish more consistency by carrying what works in one quilt into the next. At the same time, I want to resolve the problems mentioned. I have figured out what to do differently and now need to experiment to find remedies that will be consistent with my preferences as an artist. My quilt, STARS OF A DIFFERENT FEATHER, is a first step in this direction.

INSPIRATION AND DESIGN

My quilt was made specifically for the MAQS Feathered Star contest. A year ago, my design concept for this quilt was simple: a large, open star appliquéd onto a background of pieced stars that are not feathered, with curved lines of half-square triangles added to create the illusion of feathers. However, I felt that the idea was not particularly meaningful and that there could be more personal content in the design. I generated more ideas, narrowed them to five that seemed most feasible, and made color sketches of them (Figure 1).

Fig. 1. *Sketches of design ideas*

My original idea was still the best choice visually. Fortunately, while discussing the sketches and problems with my husband, he said something that triggered the title STARS OF A DIFFERENT FEATHER. It was perfect. It stated precisely what the design was doing (mixing stars and feathers), gave a focus for any needed change of visual elements, and relayed a slightly tongue-in-cheek emphasis that is "me."

For this quilt, I wanted to resolve the value and color contrast problems that were apparent in my previous work. I looked at many photos of paintings and quilts to find color combinations new to me. The one I chose felt most sophisticated: a green and brown that contained a full range of values from white to almost black. It allowed the appliqué color to complement the background while still standing out from it.

The second problem I set for myself was to use as wide a variety of star patterns as possible. I looked up Feathered Stars in every source I could find, including Marsha McCloskey's *Feathered Star Sampler* and *The Encyclopedia of Pieced Quilt Patterns* by Barbara Brackman. I ended up designing six of my own stars.

In the next twenty-four days, while cat sitting at my sister's house, I did the piecing and appliqué in fourteen- and sixteen-hour sewing days. The color-value plan was incredibly complex. For example, it required a given piece to be dark cool green while still being lighter than the piece next to it, which was also a dark cool green. The six different pieced Feathered Stars needed to be measured again and again, and altered to make the feathers and centers fit right. The six Nine-Patches of non-feathered stars were done by using templates. One of the five-sided stars had to be resewn nine times to get the final dimensions correct and still have the points right at the seam allowances. Through all of this, I had friends come visit and stay over, took a quiltmaking class, attended a high school reunion, and wandered the city eating out in restaurants and get-

ting exercise. In addition, I had to put everything away (fabric boxed, quilt rolled, machine closed) every time I was not working on it because Poochy Cat has a tendency to play with things until they are dead.

I returned home and did the quilting and finishing work in six days. The quilt has eighty-eight pieces in the appliqué and more than 1,600 pieces in the background, each cut individually from more than 300 fabrics. From the concept's design to completion, the quilt took seven weeks.

I have identified three design problems that might have been better handled if there had been more time, for example, the medium-dark brown fabric on the back. The feather quilting in the arms of the large, appliqué star is done in a dark brown thread. The meander quilting in the background is an off-white thread interspersed with five-sided stars. Had I chosen a light backing fabric, the back would have had a repeat of the large star design because the feathers would have shown well and the meander would not. Instead, I had the opposite effect.

Still, the overall quilt is the most successful one I have made. The color-value issues were resolved nicely. The piecing allows the colors to flow across the surface and yet appear as stars on close inspection. The quilt is dynamic with a strong vertical thrust that appeals to me, and from concept to completion, STARS OF A DIFFERENT FEATHER personifies the way I approach art, design, and life.

An Approach to Complex Design

I started with pencil sketches. After selecting the LeMoyne star for my appliqué, I switched to a computer drawing program. I imported the star, stretched it, then found a swirl-type texture in the program to use as the background. I tested three color schemes and chose the brown, white, and green (Figure 2, page 84).

Then curved lines were added, which were intended to be made of half-square triangle feathers, but these lines did not end up in the quilt (Figure 3). I made a copy of the background color pattern only to serve as a reference for the piecing. I used lines to separate the colors and values in the color pattern copy in much the same way that a topographical map delineates altitude changes. These area progressions are precise relative to value, color, and undertone, such as warm or cool. Then the color pattern was divided into twelve squares of 18-inch blocks and assigned either a Feathered Star pattern or a Nine-Patch, non-feathered star (Figure 4).

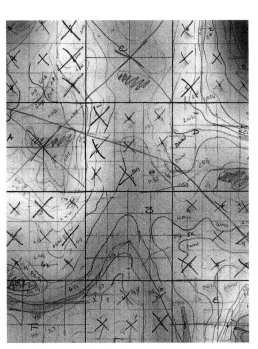

Fig. 3. *The curved lines were to be filled with feathers.*

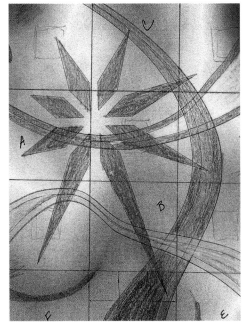

Fig. 2. *Color tests*

Fig. 4. *The colored background was printed and used for planning.*

Feathered Star: *New Quilts from an Old Favorite*

Each block was worked in sections by transferring the color areas to the block pattern and then choosing the fabrics according to not only the color pattern, but the necessary variations in value so that the star patterns would actually show (Figure 5). For instance, in the area designated light warm blue (lower left of Figure 5) there are six pieces. Of the ten fabrics I had assigned to the light warm blue stack, some that were slightly darker than the others were used for the star points. Some that were slightly lighter were used for the background, and one of the middle values was used for piece #16, part of the star's body.

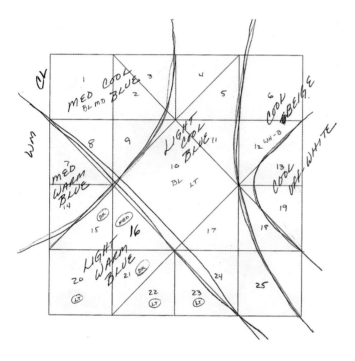

Fig. 5. *"Map" for one of the background star blocks*

I used a computer quilt design program to design the six Nine-Patches. The stars (a different one for each block) come from the program's library, with some alterations. I used the program's design grid and freehand function to draw six different five-pointed stars. These were used randomly to fill the eight outside squares in the Nine-Patches.

Key to Personal Style

The key to personal style is being consistent, specifically in these five areas:

• Visual vocabulary – the choices made regarding pattern, shape, color, and value.

• Aesthetic – the compositional principles through which the vocabulary is assembled.

• Technical approach – the media, techniques, and formats used to present the aesthetic principles.

• Content – the purpose or message that is communicated to the viewer.

• Process – the artist's method of working that mirrors, and is true to, her personality and life approach.

To develop a mature body of work, the artist must improve personal style to a level of sophistication in which every choice made is essential and supportive of the artist's intent. The goal is to have the artist's uniqueness remain inherent in the overall group of quilts produced while, at the same time, evidencing growth and change.

E-mail address for S. Cathryn Zeleny: zeleny5932@aol.com

Detail from Stars of a Different Feather

Joan Ziegler

New Port Richey, Florida

As we travel, I take many, many photographs of things that would make nice quilts some day, if I live that long.

MEET THE QUILTER

As an artist who has done oil painting, wood carving, and clay sculpture, I wanted something to do while watching television in the evening. I couldn't oil paint because that would be too messy. I couldn't carve wood because I could loose a finger, and the wood chips would be messy. Sculpting clay would be messy too. So now I quilt and have pins, needles, and fabric all over the place, but somehow that doesn't seem too messy to me.

As a self-taught quilter, I have learned much from observing other quilters. When I was three-quarters finished with my first quilt, I saw my first quilt show. I went home, finished my quilt, then gave it to the Salvation Army. I figured they wouldn't care that it looked like it had been quilted with a railroad spike. I improved after that, and my quilts got better, but not so good that I didn't cut up several to cover bushes on a frosty night in Florida.

My husband, Bob, and I have been married forty-seven years. We have two children and one grandchild, whom I spoil terribly, according to my daughter. I have made several quilts for my granddaughter. The first one, when she was an infant, was a Noah's Ark quilt for her bed, and the latest one was a Christmas quilt she can use every year to snuggle in and wait for Santa.

During the years I was painting, my husband said of every land-scape I did, "You should put a moose in there." So for his birthday I made him "Bob's Moose Quilt." He was happily surprised because I had managed to keep it a secret. Bob is an early bird, and I am a night owl, so I simply stayed up late to make the quilt. When my husband took an early retirement, we moved to Florida from Illinois. We have started to travel, and I always take some

Jacobean Fantasy

80" x 80"

quilting with me. It is a wonderful ice breaker because people will come up to ask what I am doing. One woman even brought out photos of quilts she had made, so now I carry pictures of my own quilts. As we travel, I take many, many photographs of things that would make nice quilts some day, if I live that long.

I make my quilts for my own enjoyment, but we also use them. Every time I change the bed, I change the quilt. This gives me a new look in my bedroom all the time. I have also given quilts to family members, and they use them too. It's great to go to their homes and see my quilts on their beds, especially on my granddaughter's bed. She loves to cuddle up in a quilt even in Florida's 90-degree weather.

INSPIRATION AND DESIGN

I was inspired to make JACOBEAN FANTASY after seeing Linda Roy's WINTER CHEER featured in an advertisement on the back of a quilt magazine. I loved her color choices and decided to make my own version, using the Feathered Star pattern and Jacobean flowers. The star pattern was featured in Marsha McCloskey's *Feathered Star Quilts* (Feathered Star Productions, 1987). I liked this star because the points are equally distant from each other. The Jacobean flowers were inspired by patterns in *The Best of Jacobean Appliqué* by Pat Campbell & Mimi Ayars (American Quilter's Society, 2000), but I made my own flowers and templates.

I used the needle-turn method to appliqué because it allowed me to sew while sitting in front of the television. I love the dark colors of the brown and reds in the quilt but found it rather difficult to keep the bright colors from dominating the design. I wanted the bright flowers to sparkle, not jump out and be overpowering. The trick was to use the tiniest bit of bright color and pull it all together with the greens.

I like the curved border with the tiny red touch and the ruched flowers in the Feathered Star, which were my husband's idea. I hand pieced the Feathered Stars, and the ruched flowers were made on a trip to Thailand. I found that it was so easy to pull out all the pre-cut and pre-pressed strips to stitch by hand as we traveled around by bus. I could then easily pop the pieces into my purse when we stopped, which meant there was no large sewing tote to carry.

One of the things I learned from observing other quilters' work is to put a lot of quilting in my quilts, and I love using the feather quilting pattern. Someone once told me that no space bigger than your fist should be left unquilted. I don't know if this is a rule or not, but I try to adhere to it and have found it produces very good results.

Construction of JACOBEAN FANTASY

I am a creative rather than a technical person. I do have the ability to follow written instructions, but math has always eluded me. However, I have learned a lot about math with quilting. Of course I use a calculator, but my motto is, "If in doubt, draw it out." After determining the quilt's size and deciding that the Feathered Star block would be twelve inches, my next step was drawing it on graph paper.

For the Feathered Star block, I made my own templates from old photo album pages. They work great because the drawn image will stick to one side, and the fabric will not slip on the other during cutting. If there are many pieces to trace, I use plastic template material because it is more durable.

For the center section of the quilt, the white background fabric was folded into quarters and lightly pressed. The resulting creases were used as placement guides for the appliqué. Using the templates, I drew the flower pattern in each corner. Appliquéing the Jacobean flowers to the fabric was next. The finished Feathered Star block was then appliquéd in the center, and the background fabric underneath the block was cut away.

The dark inner border was drawn on paper to create the wavy effect. I pinned the paper on my fabric and cut on the drawn line. The cut border was placed in position and hand sewn. A red ¼-inch strip was then appliquéd along the wavy edges of the border. The background fabric under the border was cut away.

The eight Jacobean border blocks were made in the same manner as the center section. These blocks were sewn to the Feathered Star blocks to make the border strips, and these were attached to the center section. The final border was made in the same manner as the first border, except I used maroon as the background instead of white. The ¼-inch red strip along the outer border was also hand sewn in place. Again, all excess fabric was removed.

The top took five to six weeks to make because I do my hand work at night, except when traveling. During the day, I do all my designing, template making, and cutting. I usually have several quilts in various stages of development at any one time.

For quilting, my husband made me a hoop that rotates 360 degrees and tilts, and I have used it for many years. Because of the Feathered Star pattern, the feather quilting pattern seemed appropriate, and it is one of my favorites. I put a grid pattern in the white background and outline quilted the flowers and other areas.

I have designed my own label, which I have used for the last several years. I use permanent, fine-point markers to draw the label, then appliqué it on the quilt back. As a last step, I photograph my quilt and catalog it so I have a record of what happens to it – was it given away, did I sell it, did it win any prizes, etc.

Detail from Jacobean Fantasy

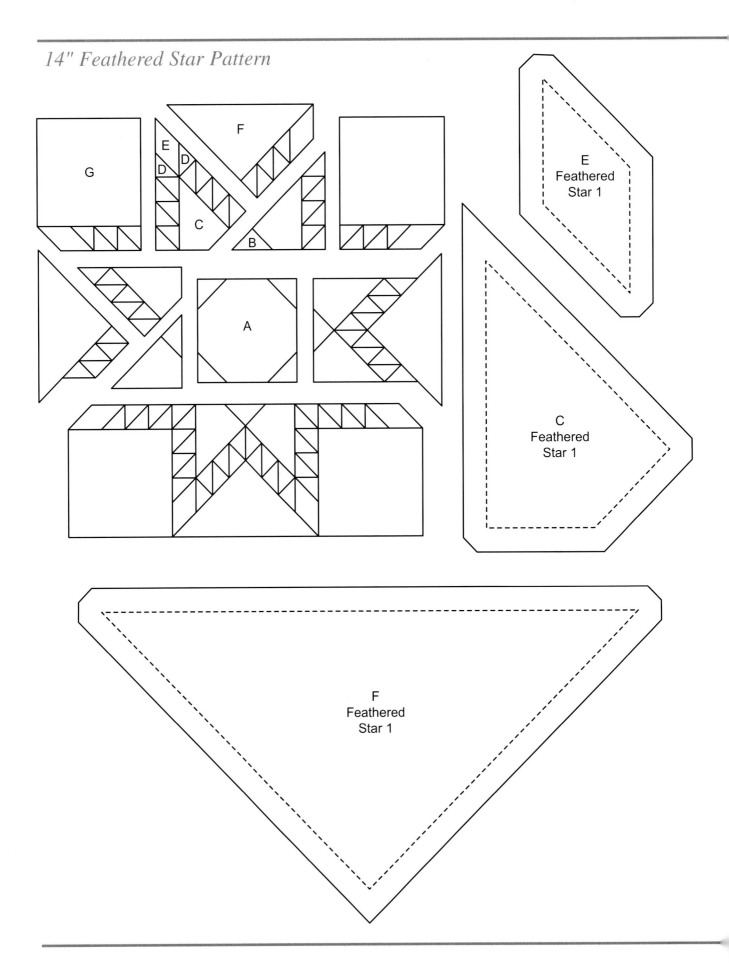

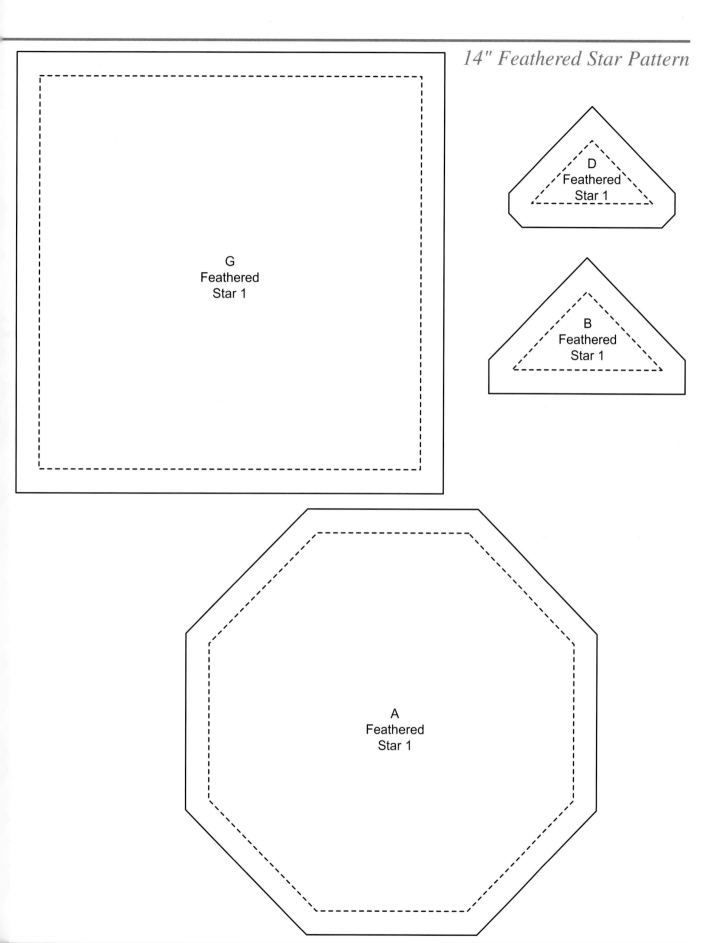

G
Feathered
Star 1

D
Feathered
Star 1

B
Feathered
Star 1

A
Feathered
Star 1

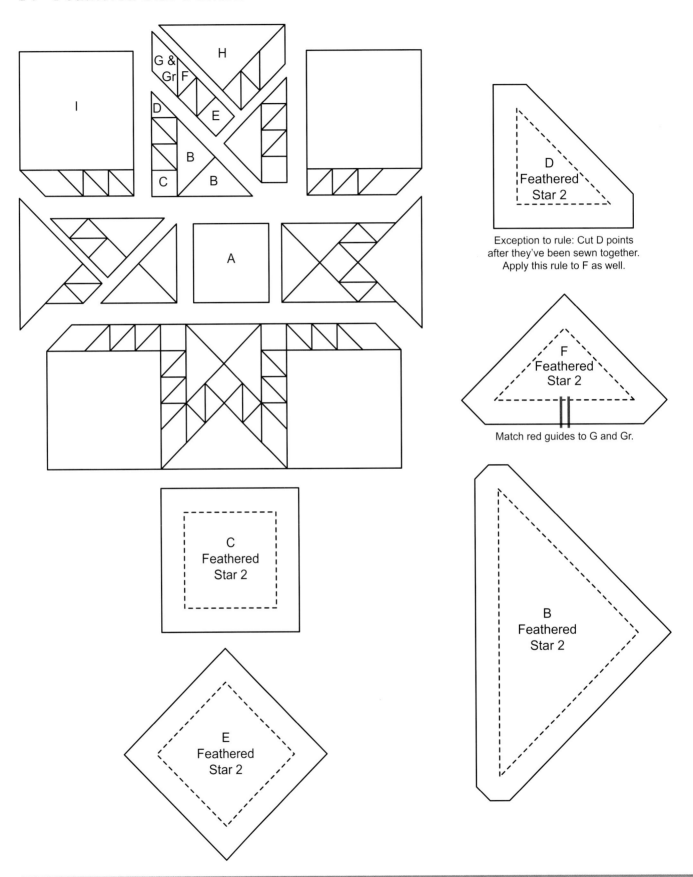

D
Feathered
Star 2

Exception to rule: Cut D points
after they've been sewn together.
Apply this rule to F as well.

F
Feathered
Star 2

Match red guides to G and Gr.

C
Feathered
Star 2

E
Feathered
Star 2

B
Feathered
Star 2

Feathered Star: *New Quilts from an Old Favorite*

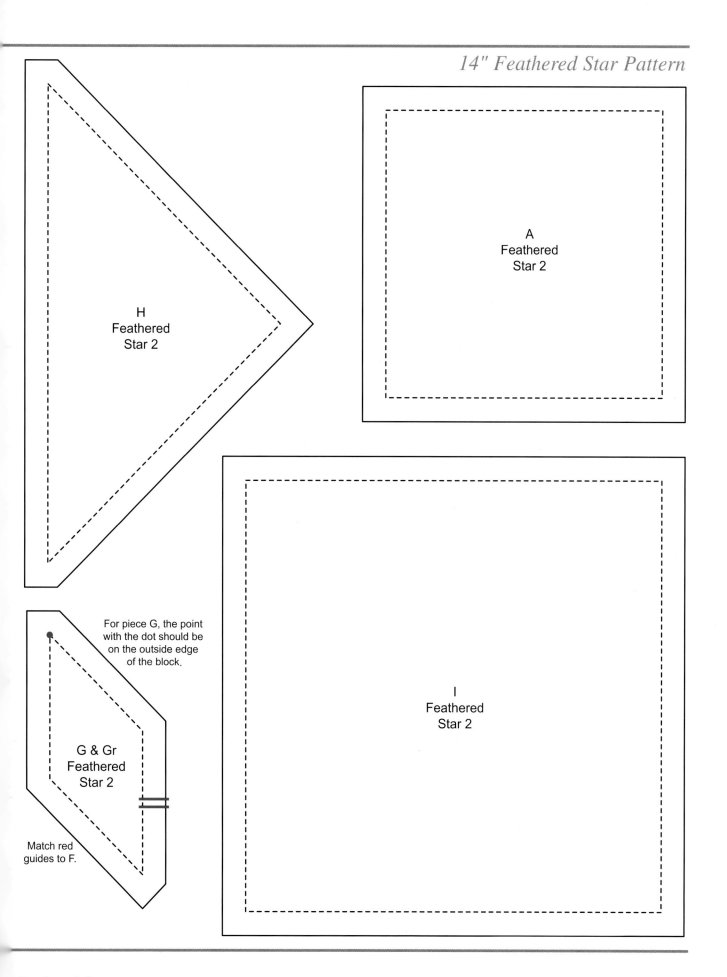

H
Feathered
Star 2

A
Feathered
Star 2

For piece G, the point
with the dot should be
on the outside edge
of the block.

G & Gr
Feathered
Star 2

I
Feathered
Star 2

Match red
guides to F.

Equal Nine-Patch

Eight-pointed Star

Unequal Nine-Patch

The Museum of the American Quilter's Society (MAQS) is an exciting place where the public can learn more about quilts, quiltmaking, and quiltmakers. Founded in 1991 by Bill and Meredith Schroeder as a not-for-profit organization, MAQS is located in an expansive 27,000 square-foot facility, making it the largest quilt museum in the world. Its facility includes three exhibit galleries, four classrooms, and a gift and book shop.

Through collecting quilts and other programs, MAQS focuses on celebrating and developing today's quiltmaking. It provides a comprehensive program of exhibits, activities, events, and services to educate about the ever-developing art and tradition of quiltmaking. Whether presenting new or antique quilts, MAQS promotes understanding of, and respect for, all quilts – new and antique, traditional and innovative, machine made and handmade, utility and art.

The MAQS exhibit galleries regularly feature a selection of the museum's own collection of quilts made from the 1980s on, as well as exhibits of new and antique quilts and related archival materials. Workshops, conferences, and exhibit-related publications provide additional educational opportunities. The museum's shop carries a wide selection of fine crafts and hundreds of quilt and textile books.

Located in historic downtown Paducah, Kentucky, MAQS is open year-round 10 A.M. to 5 P.M. Monday through Saturday. From April 1 through October 31, it is also open on Sundays from 1 to 5 P.M. The entire facility is wheelchair accessible.

MAQS programs can also be enjoyed on the website: www.quiltmuseum.org or through MAQS traveling exhibits, like the *New Quilts from an Old Favorite* contest and exhibit. For more information, write MAQS, PO Box 1540, Paducah, KY 42002-1540; phone (270) 442-8856; or e-mail: info@quiltmuseum.org.

Other AQS Books

This is only a small selection of the books available from the American Quilter's Society. AQS books are known worldwide for timely topics, clear writing, beautiful color photos, and accurate illustrations and patterns. The following books are available from your local bookseller, quilt shop, or public library.

#6036   us$24.95

#5754   us$19.95

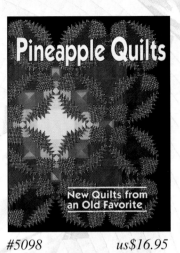

#5098   us$16.95

#5852   us$19.95

#6078   us$19.95

#5592   us$19.95

#5883   us$24.95

#6005   us$19.95

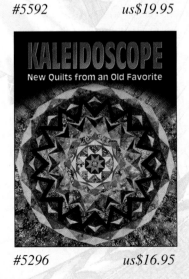

#5296   us$16.95